Immersion

Immersion

A Pilgrimage into Service

James Menkhaus

New City Press
Hyde Park, New York

Published by New City Press
202 Comforter Blvd.,
Hyde Park, NY 12538
www.newcitypress.com

Immersion: A Pilgrimage into Service
James Menkhaus

Cover design and layout by Miguel Tejerina

Library of Congress Control Number: 2021921097

ISBN 978-1-56548-710-9 (paperback)
ISBN 978-1-56548-711-6 (e-book)
Printed in the United States of America

Contents

To Fr. Howard Gray, in gratitude
for your wisdom, guidance, and friendship.
Rest in Peace 5-7-18

Acknowledgments

It is impossible to adequately express my gratitude to all whose voices speak through these pages. My own pilgrimage into international service began in 2009 when I was invited by Helen and Patrick Rombalski to present at an orientation program for *Rostro de Cristo* and the international Jesuit Volunteers. This was, in many ways, the beginning of conversations and experiences that are the essence of this book. I continued to present at orientations for these programs until the COVID-19 pandemic of 2020 put their work on hold. I am also indebted to the Ignatian Solidarity Network, the Humility of Mary Volunteer Program, and Hope for Honduran Children. These organizations have offered me opportunities to learn and grow in my understanding of service and justice. I am grateful for the support of John Carroll University, Gannon University, and Gilmour Academy for the opportunities to teach and/or travel with their students. These experiences have helped me become more attuned to the needs of the readers of this book who are undergoing immersive service experiences. While I greatly appreciate the opportunities afforded me by these institutions, the views expressed in this manuscript are my own. It should not be assumed that these organizations agree with everything I say here.

In terms of the text itself, I am especially grateful to Paula Fitzgerald, Martha Ligas, Sean Cahill, and Cortney Freshwater, who read each chapter of the manuscript as it was written and offered ideas for critiques, edits, and improvements. Their input was invaluable. I also appreciate the efforts of Eric Abercrombie, Kat Rankin, Nicole Bubie, Francis Boccuzzi, and Bri Lazarchik, who read selections and offered thoughts and suggestions that became part of the final manuscript.

I would like to acknowledge those who helped guide the trajectory of early proposals for the book. Ed Hahnenberg, Jeff Bloodworth, Abbey Vogel, Evan Cuthbert, Andy Costigan, and Paul Lauritzen helped me think through ways to integrate the immersion material in the current context of our country and the world. Meredith Mallon-Jeffrey and Jorja Hlifka rekindled my love of writing during the early stages of the pandemic. I do not think I would have written the book if not for the inspiration of our writing group. Finally, I wish to thank my parents for their love and support. Although they are not fluent in the language of immersion and service, they supported my goals and experiences that made this exploration possible.

This book is dedicated to Fr. Howard Gray, who died tragically in a car accident in 2018. He was a dear friend and second father to me for nearly fifteen years.

He planted the spiritual seeds in my life that germinated into the person I have become. This book would not exist without his tutelage and love.

Preface

High school assemblies are rarely the highlight of a student's day. However, a class meeting during my junior year at St. Xavier High School in Cincinnati, Ohio, set me on a path that I am still traveling today. I went into the assembly thankful for missing class and getting out of the heat of a warm spring day, but I left with a new understanding of service. That was the day I first heard about "mission trips." My white middle-class bubble was shaken.

I only recall a few details from that meeting, such as pictures of Latin American families and the stories some of the seniors told about their experiences encountering poverty. Sure, I was aware that people in the world were hungry or didn't have a home. But "those people" were far removed from my experiences. Now, I was hearing stories from my classmates who had encountered people in these situations in other countries. They talked about their faith and how they saw God in these relationships. My heartbeat quickened as my mind whirled with possibilities. I sat back and thought, "I could do this too . . ."

Upon arriving home that evening I immediately shared this new excitement with my parents. I told them I wanted to go on one of these international trips and that I wanted to help people. My parents, however, saw things differently. My mother reminded me that such travel would be impossible because of my medical condition, cystic fibrosis (CF). She pointed out that people with CF can't travel to areas where health facilities are not "modernized" and easily accessible. My heart began to sink. My father then objected on other grounds. "One of your relatives went to Appalachia to help the poor and they told her to turn around and go home," he muttered. "They don't want you there," he soundly concluded, while barely looking up from reading the evening newspaper.

I left dinner and sat in my room defeated. Perhaps my father was correct, and these trips were a waste of time. I wasn't sure how to respond to him. I was more certain, however, that my mother was correct. I missed school all the time for illness, so the reality that I physically could not participate in a "mission trip" became solidified in my mind. Service trips became something that was for other people. When I heard students describe their experiences "working with the poor" it hardened my position and embittered my relationship with God. I thought, "Why doesn't God want me to have these types of experiences too?" During college retreat presentations I ignored service stories because listening made me feel a sense of guilt that I was not healthy enough to help people on service trips, and anger toward that weakness.

The objections voiced by my parents are among the common concerns of parents who are confronted with their child's initial excitement for going on a service or immersion trip or for entering postgraduate volunteer programs. My parents are very loving people, but they were not exposed to the experience that I was proposing, and their comments went unchallenged in my mind for many years. I was equally unprepared to respond in a healthy way that demonstrated the reasons I wanted to go on such a trip and the types of safety precautions in place. Their objections became my resentment. It was not until ten years later that I gained the self-confidence to attempt an immersion experience. I served as a faculty accompanier on a week-long immersion to Louisville, Kentucky. Participation in this event began to undo the years of disappointment that I had inappropriately directed toward myself.

Through this book I hope to offer a response to parents and other people who struggle with the merits of service immersion experiences or wonder about the balance of risks and benefits. We will explore connections between faith and justice, contemplation and action, isolation and immersion, by using an Ignatian[1] framework. Two underlying questions throughout the text will be: 1) What does it mean to say *you* are called to enter the reality of another? and 2) What does it mean to go to the *place* of another, to immerse yourself in that reality? By applying theology,

---

1. "Ignatian" refers to the spirituality of St. Ignatius of Loyola, a sixteenth-century Spanish mystic who founded the Society of Jesus, also known as the Jesuits.

Ignatian spirituality, and storytelling, as well as my own experiences working with volunteers and being touched by their lives, I hope to offer a response. The critiques voiced by my parents and others are important and should not be summarily dismissed. In fact, there are many layers of unhealthy applications of power and privilege that should be explored before partaking in service experiences. These discussions are crucial to avoid cultural and racial hegemony that perpetuates the injustices already present in these marginalized communities. This book is not meant to conclude the discussion, but to reframe it using an Ignatian paradigm and to invite further discussion.

By using examples from my own pilgrimage and those of others, I will invite you, the reader, to examine your own journey. Whether you are interested in participating for a week, a year, or more time of intentional and immersive service, or you have a loved one with these aspirations, I hope this book offers tools for your reflection. If you are currently engaged in a service experience, or have a friend who is, I hope this book helps you reflect on what is happening. And if you have returned from a service experience and potentially see the world in a new way, I hope this book helps you make sense of your experience. You are not on this journey alone. There are no simple answers to these questions, but the answer is not to ignore the question. The invitation is to "live into" the ambiguity of the question.

To Give Your Heart to God

Fr. Howard Gray, SJ, whose stories and insights are embedded in this book, was an internationally known Jesuit who served in numerous positions at Jesuit universities and within the Jesuit order until his death in 2018.[2] While leading a retreat in 2015 he shared the following story in a homily. Father Gray had been assigned, as a young Jesuit, to minister to an elderly nun who was in the final stages of her life. He sat by her bedside daily as she reflected on her life and the lessons she had learned from her ministry. One day she told him that when the church had asked her to go back to school, to learn and earn a degree, she did so freely and without hesitation. She explained that she was being asked to give her "mind to God." Many years later, she was asked to become a superior of a school. She had never sought this

---

2. Some of Father Gray's positions included: rector of the Weston Jesuit School of Theology in Massachusetts, provincial of the Jesuits' Detroit Province (1983–1989), director of the Center for Ignatian Spirituality at Boston College, assistant to the president at John Carroll University, and assistant to the president for special projects at Georgetown University. He was killed in a car accident in May 2018 at the age of eighty-seven.

role, but accepted it without reservation. The church, she explained, was asking her to give her "hands to God," to build a strong school so students could attend for years to come. She then paused her story and reflected. "But Father," she said, "while I was giving my mind to God and my hands to God, I never stopped to ask myself if I was giving my heart to God. What God truly wants is not your mind, nor your hands. God wants your heart. And, when you discover how to give your heart to God, do it every day."

Ultimately, this book is about discovering how to give your heart to God. Yes, it is about service and immersion work. Yes, it is about finding ways to give your mind to God through teaching, or your hands to God through service. But if you neglect the most important component of this work, giving your heart to God, then the true purpose of these good works will fall short. Work for justice, solidarity, inclusion, and equality should never focus on the one working for change. It should always lead us outward, to the God of love, who gives life and nourishment to our work for justice. Just as Jesus never made His mission about Himself, so, too, we must rise above that temptation, always checking if we are giving our hearts to God.

The Structure, Timing, and Purpose of this Book

First and foremost, this is a book of narratives from my life. It is also informed by stories from those who have done or are doing service work, as well as key figures in the Christian tradition. As a college professor I participated in numerous immersion trips with students. I have also traveled to Ecuador and Tanzania to lead retreats for volunteers who were engaged in service through international volunteer programs based in the United States. The stories come predominantly from these experiences. Insights of students, volunteers, campus ministers, activists, teachers, religious, and others are at the heart of the book.

I have thought about writing this book for ten years. It was not until the COVID-19 pandemic and the racial justice awakening in the United States during the summer of 2020 that I coalesced my notes into this text. Two thousand twenty will be remembered as a year of change, and hopefully, these changes will lead people to a stronger appreciation of the value of all human life. Immersion and service work will also be affected by 2020. Some people will ultimately ask, Why should I leave the United States when there is so much work to be done in this country in pursuit of justice and equality? This book will not try to convince you to do one thing or the other. Rather, it will invite you to look inside yourself to see where God is calling you to share your gifts and talents with the world. We are all called to work for justice, whether in our hearts, in our country, or around the globe.

Catholic high schools and universities were steadily increasing their number of service and immersion programs prior to the pandemic. With the current emphasis on assessing educational experiences inside and outside the classroom, immersion "success" seems difficult to quantify. Should schools continue to support these programs? Is this the best use of funds? Are these experiences actually just glorified study abroad programs that are self-centered in their focus? Assessing the validity of these programs for institutions and individuals will be even more important in the post-COVID-19 world. While this book is not directed toward those goals, hopefully it will contribute meaningfully to the conversations about what qualifies as a "successful" service experience.

Given that context, each chapter contains insights from Scripture and theology. I hope these sections help to concretize the theological topic of each chapter in a way that is reflective and helpful. Within each part is also an insight from the life of Fr. Pedro Arrupe, SJ, who served as the superior general of the Society of Jesus from 1965–1983. Arrupe's life and teachings were instrumental as the Society of Jesus refocused itself toward issues of justice and immersion work following Vatican II. I hope that this book will not only serve as an opportunity for people to reflect on their own narrative but also introduce them to the life of Arrupe in an authentic and engaging way.

I use "immersion" to refer to any service trip where a person is taken into the culture or life of another for a period of time. This may be for direct service, accompaniment, or a combination of both. Study abroad programs which focus on learning languages or tourist experiences can certainly include service and accompaniment, but these trips are not my focus. I hope, however, that many of the topics covered here would be applicable for these "education-based" programs as well. These distinctions are not mine to make and can be evaluated on a case-by-case basis by the individual who is preparing for or undergoing the experience.

I am using the term "immersion" instead of "missionary work" because of the stigma that can be attached to the term "missionary." I think this is an unfortunate stereotype, because "mission language" does not have to be connected to colonialism. When Evan Cuthbert took over for the *Rostro de Cristo*³ program as executive director in 2013, he led a session on missiology at the combined Jesuit Volunteer Corps International⁴ and *Rostro de Cristo* orientation. During the presentation he asked the volunteers to consider how they feel being labeled as "missioners," a term he adopted while working as a Catholic missionary in Bolivia. His intention was to challenge them to consider a term beyond "volunteer" that encompassed a faith component. The volunteers struggled with the description of

---

3. *Rostro de Cristo*, translated as Face of Christ, was founded by Fr. Jim Ronan in 1989. The organization invites young people to serve in Ecuador, typically for one year. They host retreat groups from colleges and high schools around the country who are introduced to the reality of life in impoverished areas of Ecuador.

4. The Jesuit Volunteer Corps began in 1956 when college students served in Alaska. According to their website, they have over eleven thousand alumni around the world. More information can be found at *www.jesuitvolunteers.org/history*.

themselves as missioners because of the similarity to "missionary." These volunteers were preparing to go to Ecuador, Micronesia, Tanzania, Chile, Nicaragua, Belize, and Peru. Many of these countries had been colonized by people who came as "missionaries," and the volunteers feared that using this language would perpetuate a stereotype of inequality and aggression.

The following year, Evan explored the idea of being a "missioner" more deeply. He focused on living the mission of the Gospel, clearly articulating that the Gospel is an invitation to a way of life. Encountering people living on the margins means choosing to live out the mission of the Gospel in a radical way. The difference between the terms continues to be a touchy subject each year at orientation. In order to sidestep important discussions within this tension, all service and accompaniment experiences will be referred to in this book as "immersions" or "immersive service experiences," and those who participate as "volunteers."

This book is divided into six parts, each containing three chapters. At the end of each chapter are reflection questions that will hopefully help you in your discernment or reflection. Some questions are for individual consideration, while others could be helpful to discuss with your immersion group or community. All questions are designed to spur reflection and do not have definite right or wrong answers. The first two parts could be used prior to an immersion or postgraduate service experience. Parts three, four, and five are designed for those currently undergoing an immersive service experience. The final part invites reflection on integrating the lessons learned from service into the rest of your life. While the application of all of the material will vary from person to person, the culminating part is especially unique to each individual.

One of the catchphrases of Ignatian spirituality is "finding God in all things." This spiritual insight includes moments of awe, challenging conversations, experiences of love and gratitude, and times of struggle. We are invited to ask ourselves daily, "How is God working in this situation?" Sometimes, "finding God in all things" will be easier while engaging in direct service to others. The elderly nun who offered advice to Father Gray in the opening story of the introduction found it easy to give her mind and hands to God, but realized only later that God wanted her heart. In other words, it was easier to understand God's call and presence in the physical activities of her ministry. You will likely experience this in the encounters you have during service. These moments of grace could offer you ample opportunity to open your eyes to the presence of God in all things. But the challenge is also to go further. As you discover God in all of creation, search for a way to give your heart to God. Try to move the idea of "finding God in all things" from daily service opportunities to a more intimate understanding of your relationship with God. This will push you deeper and challenge you in ways that are unpredictable. And when you discover how to do that, do it every day—not just during your time of service, but for the rest of your life. Service isn't the beginning or the end of your pilgrimage. However, it may be an important step that will transform your life forever.

Part One

The Principle and the Foundation

I always ate hot dogs with ketchup as a child. So, when I was getting two hot dogs for someone I had never met, I assumed ketchup was the go-to condiment. Sure, I recognize that there are far more healthy things to eat, and no one truly knows what is in a hot dog, but that is beside the point. And in this case, there were no other options. The meal I held in my hand was lukewarm, likely heated over an hour ago. The cold climate certainly didn't help matters. A light snow fell on my face as I made my way across the encampment of those experiencing homelessness. It was November in Cleveland, Ohio, so a cold evening was commonplace, but it felt like the coldest night of the year. Perhaps I was shivering from the cold, or perhaps it was because I am an introvert and was about to speak to someone I had never met. At one point I knew the name of the man whose home I was approaching, but this was over fifteen years ago. His name is no longer part of my memory, but our encounter is etched on my heart.

The first part of this book is built upon recollection. If you are discerning a year of service or participation in an immersion program, I invite you to reflect on the stories and insights that follow and ask yourself if you have a similar story. If so, I invite you to explore that narrative and start to answer the first question of the preface: Why might *I* be called to service—to enter the reality of another? This begins with an inward gaze into the human being that you are by tracing the part of your narrative that led you to this point. Then, ask yourself: What are the non-negotiable elements of my personality that elicit a desire to serve? In the first chapter, we will establish a theological basis for exploring narrative. In the second, this basis will be applied to the Gospel passage of the man born blind (John 9). The final chapter of this part will apply these concepts to stories of service and immersion in order to give you the opportunity to make these connections in your own life.

Chapter 1

Narrative, Imagination, and Memory

In order to share the hot dog story with you I needed to use my memory. I am not in touch with anyone else who was involved in that experience, so the recollection came solely from me. I drew on my imagination to reconstruct this experience in my mind. By "imagination," I do not mean that the story is fictional. It is an event that happened as I recall it. I remember some details, such as the cold air and the warmth of the food against my hand. But like other past events, it continues to exist in the minds of those who experienced it. In this case, there were no cameras or videos. It was long before Snapchat and Instagram. This reconstruction could be classified as a secular examination of the past, retold for your pleasure or interest. However, one can contend that both the telling and the reading are also spiritual experiences, and that storytelling can have a meaning deeper than a regurgitation of facts. To explore this concept more deeply, we will briefly examine the connection between spirituality and narrative, imagination, and memory.

Narrative is a way of communicating human experience. The Bible, early writings of the desert fathers and mothers, the stories of the saints, and tales of conversions are narratives of human experience. As I reflect on a story over time, the meaning I draw from it may change depending on the experiences of my life at that time. Certainly, retelling the story where I delivered hot dogs the day after it happened generated a different focus on detail, a different style of telling it, and a different interpretation of what it meant for my life than it did as I was writing this book. We do not tell stories of our lives only once, in a static manner. We tell them repeatedly. Based on audience, intention, and subsequent experience, the story can be told differently each time.

"Imagination" usually conjures up images of the fanciful. Children are taught to use their imaginations to construct realities that are fictional or aspirational. However, spirituality and memory need the imagination to create an environment for the reconstruction of past events. Even while being as honest as one can be, there is always room for perspective. I, as the interpreter of my own memory, am constructing the past experience with integrity in the world that no longer physically exists. Thus, the landscape for narrative exploration needs the imagination to fuel re-creation.

Memory is also crucial to giving meaning to narrative. Memory allows the past to become present again, whether in the mind of an individual or in those who hear the narrative retold. In order to understand the importance of memory, we can look to the use of a storytelling technique that is often employed in cinema. Movies like *Forrest Gump* move the story forward by having a character retell past experiences. A lesser-known movie that employs this technique is *Cinema Paradiso*, a story about a middle-aged Italian filmmaker. Much of the movie is seen through his eyes as he looks back on the formative moments of his youth, growing up in a small town under the tutelage of a movie projectionist. In the final scene of the movie, the present (as established by the opening scene) continues as the now-older man returns to the town where much of the movie—his memories—took place. He opens a gift from the now-deceased projectionist and finds a series of film clips that had been cut out of films that were shown in the town. Because the local priest had wanted to avoid scandal, he had forced the projectionist to remove romantic scenes. The protagonist weeps while the clips roll, as the realities of his past and present converge in a reflection on who he has become. Seeing these depictions of love also calls to mind his own struggles to find a romantic connection with another person.

Cinema Paradiso is, in some ways, the story of many of us. We look back at our lives, only to arrive in the present after sifting through these memories to try to make meaning of our past. How did I become who I am today? The filmmaker was overcome by the memory of the tenderness and care from the old projectionist. This love, embodied in those final clips of romance, is an invitation not only to the character, but also to the viewer. By retelling our stories, we are invited to reflect on the story of the other and on our own story. Where in our lives have we experienced love (perhaps in the form of a mentor, like the protagonist of *Cinema Paradiso*)? Where have we experienced—or avoided—romantic love? What does the viewing or hearing of this story in the present awaken in my own memory? And, in this act of retelling, how can I come to know where God was during this time? Memory is both affective and effective: affective in forming who I am; effective in inviting the one listening to or reading the story to reflect on their own journey.

Looking at these three elements together—narrative, imagination, and memory—a case can be made that God communicates to us through our imagination. This is certainly a central feature of the *Spiritual Exercises* of St. Ignatius. This retreat relies on examining our narrative in light of the narrative of Jesus. The goal is to uncover and discern the way God is working in our lives. More will be said in part two concerning discernment. For now, I submit that our stories matter, not just to us, but also in the life of the Spirit. Retelling our stories to others and to ourselves is not just an exercise in nostalgia, but an opportunity for renewed examination and articulation into the way we are touched by mystery. Our narratives are not ours alone. They are experienced with others and with God. If God wants to be known, as the Christian tradition holds, our narratives are an important place to search out the God who wishes to dwell among us, and we should use the tools of imagination and memory to give form to this formless mystery.

Storytelling and Imperfection

It is also important to examine storytelling in the context of imperfection and mistakes. In their book *The Spirituality of Imperfection*, Ernest Kurtz and Katherine Ketcham draw upon a myriad of insights into the importance of storytelling to spirituality and apply those to what they call the "most tragic human mistake." The mistake is trying to be perfect. Striving for perfection can be debilitating. It might hold a person back from trying something new or from taking a risk because the person knows that it may not turn out with the perfect or intended result. However, this spiritual insight also speaks to the past as we examine our narratives using our memory. At times, one does not like what one finds. This may be the case as you move toward examining your own motivations for service work. Fortunately, perspectives like those offered in *The Spirituality of Imperfection* remind us to balance who we want to be with the person we are, mistakes and all.

In establishing the importance of narrative, Kurtz and Ketcham explain that people of ancient times told stories to celebrate and mourn experiences in life. Stories are methods for making meaning out of our lives, whether positive or negative. The authors explain, "Without imperfection's 'gap between intentions and results' there would be no story."[5] Thus, we should not hide from the failings of our past or from difficult stories that make us

---

5. Ernest Kurtz and Katherine Ketcham, *The Spirituality of Imperfection: Storytelling and the Search for Meaning* (New York: Bantam Books, 1993), 7.

look bad, as those, too, could be invitations to dig deeper into ourselves. The telling of our stories is a sacred event, a sharing of who we are. This sharing may be directed toward ourselves in reflection or toward those we trust with our inner selves.

As you examine your narrative in connection with your desire to serve, it is possible that you may uncover embarrassing experiences in your memory, or mistakes you made which you would rather bury deep in the recesses of your mind. But these moments are just as important to your identity as times of triumph or insight. For example, a person who once held racist views or told homophobic jokes may have awakened to the reality of the pain they caused others. Or perhaps you uncover moments when you were not charitable toward people who held different views. You may have perceived these perspectives as offensive or harmful without actually engaging the person in dialogue. Yes, it is important to reconstruct the moments of realization in your imagination, but that is not a complete picture of your identity. Reconstructing those times when you were not perfect or when you did something hurtful may help you better discern who you want to be or how to help others have a clarity of vision in how to work for justice. Kurtz and Ketcham remind us of those imperfect realties and the importance of authentically claiming parts of ourselves that we would rather forget.

Whether I am teaching a high school or a college course, I begin by assigning the introduction to *The Spirituality of Imperfection*. Students often come into a required theology course with strong feelings—either in favor of theology or against it. In some cases, their hesitation toward religious or spiritual ideas is from a sense of "unworthiness." Inviting students to realize that we do not measure God's love of us through a lens of "worthiness" can be a difficult task. God does not decide who is worthy of love; God offers love to all. It is not about finding oneself worthy, but about affirming oneself as a loved creature. I ask students to look at their story and to detect where these "lack of worth" feelings originated.

A number of years ago during a Christmas Eve family gathering I asked my cousin Stacie if she would like to join me for midnight Mass. She was raised Catholic and attended Mass in her youth, but as a young adult she rarely went to church. I thought she would simply decline the offer. However, in a sad tone, she reflected, "No thanks, I don't think God wants me there." It wasn't glib or sarcastic, but a reflective statement that I felt she was processing as she said it. While I assured her that God "wanted her there" just as much as God wanted me there, she ultimately demurred. The exchange has stuck with me, and I wonder how often my students come into a theology course believing that God doesn't care about them. Often, there is something in their narrative, their story, that established this harmful self-doubt about the love of God. Understanding that we are not perfect is important when we go back into our memory. While those *are* your memories, you are no longer the person you were, and you should proceed gently through the array of your previous experiences.

As I dug into the recesses of my mind to share the story that opened part one, I had to revisit parts of myself that I wished I could change. As I mentioned in the preface, I was once inhibited by the belief that immersion programs were not for me. Because of my medical condition, I closed my mind to being called to service. This showed not only my stubbornness, but also a limited understanding of theology. I eventually participated in the program that led me to the streets of Cleveland to offer food and fellowship to people experiencing homelessness. While I had a lot of hesitation and fear, as well as anger toward and disappointment in myself, I decided to try the experience.

This is the context in which I carried hot dogs across the encampment on a cold November evening while I was working at John Carroll University. I joined the students in the van that was designated "west side." At one of our stops we parked in a deserted area under a bridge where approximately ten individuals lived in tents. My heart pounded as I was told to deliver hot dogs and juice to a man living in a box on the far side of the encampment. I was shaking from the cold and could see my breath in the evening air. But perhaps more, I was shaking from fear of the coming encounter. Would this man see me as a nuisance? A spoiled rich kid coming to give him a small meal? He was sitting partially inside the box, trying to keep warm. As I stepped forward and reached out, I looked down at where I was standing. The flap of the box was open and I was standing on it. As he said "thank you," it hit me that I was not standing on a box, but on this man's home. Perhaps this flap was his doormat and I was not offending him. Or maybe I was standing on one of the few things he owned. I awkwardly moved my foot to the side and continued to converse with him.

I do not remember what we said, but as I walked away a few moments later I thought of my apartment. I thought of how I would not be cold that night and how I could get a warm meal whenever I wished. This man didn't have opportunities to sleep in a warm bed or access an abundance of food. I was filled with sadness, rage, confusion, and, most of all, guilt. I can look back at this experience now to see it as a foundational moment that broke me out of my self-centered wariness of service. I can recall it in my memory and am able, now, to be gentle with myself about the way I felt and about my understanding of justice. In order to better understand how to extrapolate God's presence from this snapshot we will turn to the Gospel in chapter 2.

Reflection Questions

1. Have you had an experience like that of my cousin, who felt that God did not want her at church? Or, have you had a time when you felt unworthy of God's love? Where do you think these feelings originated?

2. Is there a memory that causes you to feel guilt around your desire to work for justice or a memory that affirms your desire to work for justice?

Chapter 2

The Man Born Blind

One way to describe the Gospels is as a collection of stories. This does not mean they did not happen. It simply means that narratives are intertwined among the parables and teachings of Jesus. In John 9, Jesus and his disciples encounter a man who was born blind. Upon seeing this man, the disciples inquire if the blindness is a punishment for the wrongs of the man or of his parents. While this sounds like an odd inquiry, it was not out of place for Jesus' disciples to believe this. Jesus explains that neither the man nor his parents sinned. Rather, his condition exists so that the works of God might be made visible through him. It is not that Jesus is saying the man was born blind because God wanted a test subject for Jesus to perform a miracle. The man is blind. Jesus, through his love, will give him sight.

When the Pharisees, who are often portrayed in the New Testament as strict adherents to Jewish law, hear about the cure, they accuse the man of fraudulent begging. They believe he could not ever have been blind because now he can see. After they repeatedly interrogate him about what he believes about the stranger who cured him, the man proclaims that he does not know if that man is a sinner. He only knows he was blind and now he can see. The miracle is not only about the restoration of sight to a man born blind. It is about changing the way we see those who are blind. Jesus affirms through this cure event that abnormalities at birth are not punishments for sin.

Just as the man born blind proclaims that he was blind, but now sees, so too are people blind to the realities of the world, believing poverty and illness are the fault of individuals. The predominant notion that one needs only to work hard to succeed fails to take account of external forces, personal difficulties, systems of oppression, and the survival impulse that leaves neighbors fighting over scarce goods. The first step toward removing these obstacles is vision. A problem cannot be solved if it isn't known to exist. If the poverty of another is neatly hidden away, or the ill and elderly who cannot afford medical care are left alone, no one is aware of these injustices.

And Now I See

As a way of tying together the insights of Kurtz and Ketcham on storytelling and the message of this Gospel passage, we turn to Bishop Robert Barron's book *And Now I See*. In his introduction, Barron explains that the purpose of his book is to show "*how* theological doctrines, dogmas, and stories function 'metanoetically,' how they transform souls."[6] Drawing upon a wide-ranging array of literature, philosophy, and theology, Barron teases out transformational components of these works. Christ gave sight to the man born blind; just so, Barron contends, these works in the Christian tradition present "an icon of Christ and hence an agent for the transformation of souls and the opening up of vision."[7] For Barron, Christianity is ultimately a way of seeing, and narrative demonstrates the power of vision through the eyes of Christ, the one who opened the eyes of the man born blind.

A central concept to Barron's book is that of *metanoia*, the changing of perspective through the opening of the eyes, leading one from the *pusilla anima* (small soul) to the *magna anima* (great soul). The small soul is self-absorbed and dominated by ego, while the great soul surrenders in trust to God. The call for invitation and rebirth, for God to be with us, arises from the *magna anima*, transforming us into the *imago Dei*, the image of God. This is the transformation of the soul which opens the eyes to the reality of what is around us. Echoing the importance of narrative found in Kurtz and Ketcham, Barron explains that we must look inside ourselves with honesty at the story of our lives.

Barron uses a multitude of authors and writings in the Christian tradition that demonstrate the journey toward Christ's call to see with new eyes. One of these figures is Thomas Merton. Barron contends that Merton's autobiog-

---

6.   Robert Barron, *And Now I See: A Theology of Transformation* (New York: Crossroad Publishing, 1998), 14.

7.   Barron, *Now I See*, 16.

raphy, *Seven Story Mountain*, demonstrates the movement of the soul toward God. Barron writes: "One must allow [the *imago Dei*] to grow and unfold like a seed in the soil of the soul. Once the buried treasure has been found, everything must be sold so the field can be bought."[8] Merton's foundational experience at Fourth and Walnut in Louisville, Kentucky, is an incredible realization of God's love. Merton walked away from this street corner believing he saw people as God sees them—as loved, and shining like the sun. For Barron, this experience is a beautiful indication of the *imago Dei*: a movement from self-focus to the realization of the love and presence of God in all people— the blossoming of the *magna anima*.

While the story of the man born blind in John 9 is only one example of a narrative in the Christian tradition, it is a powerful one. As we read and reread this passage, it can speak to us in different ways. Like any narrative, our condition when hearing it partly dictates what we pull from it. Like *Forrest Gump* or *Cinema Paradiso*, the story invites us to apply the themes to our own lives. How are we blind to Christ? In what ways can we undergo a metanoia from the *pusilla anima* to the *magna anima* to further be the *imago Dei* in the world? In recalling the past through our memory, we are called to place ourselves into the narrative in order to more clearly see that which is inside of us. This may reveal moments of social justice progress or difficult experiences of denial of God's love for all people. In the

---

8. Barron, *Now I See*, 65.

final chapter of this part, we will turn to a few snapshots from the memory of Fr. Pedro Arrupe, a former superior general of the Society of Jesus. These experiences not only dramatically altered his narrative, but also draw us into finally asking which of *our* narratives may function in this manner: as a call to metanoia.

Reflection Questions

1. Jesus gave sight to the man born blind. Are there areas of justice work that you can identify that you were once blind to, but now can see? How were you made aware of these realities?

2. What is your image of God? Can you represent this image in a picture or poem?

Chapter 3

A Hungry Boy

In 1965 Pedro Arrupe entered the highest levels of governance in the Society of Jesus (Jesuits) as the superior general. But, long before that, he was a medical student at the University of Madrid from 1923–1927. Although he was not from the wealthy class, Arrupe's contact with poverty was minimal during his youth. When one of the older students founded a branch of the St. Vincent de Paul Society for medical students interested in helping the poor, Arrupe volunteered to join.

Arrupe specifically recalls an encounter that helped concretize his desires to leave medical school. He met a young boy who was eating a roll in the middle of the afternoon. He approached the boy and inquired why he was eating a snack that would ruin his dinner. When the boy told him that it was not a snack, but rather his only meal of the day, Arrupe was shocked. The boy continued to explain that he did not have a father and that his mother was the only one caring for his needs. Arrupe never forgot the boy's face and his own experience of personally encountering a child's hunger for the first time.[9]

Arrupe had another powerful experience of poverty during his time in medical school. He and a friend visited a widow in a poor neighborhood of Vallecas in Spain. They found six children and two widows living in one room. All eight of them slept on the same mattress. They did not have enough clothing to stay warm and they shared a blanket. Arrupe and his friend walked home in silence. Like the encounter with the young boy with bread, Arrupe never forgot the experience of seeing these women and children huddled together in one small apartment, lacking the food and resources appropriate to their human dignity.[10]

Pedro Arrupe's early contact with social injustice generated a new purpose within his soul. How Arrupe enacted his role as superior general should not be divorced from his formative experiences during medical school. Jesuit institutions often praise Arrupe's speech "Men and Women for Others," which he delivered in 1973, as foundational to the contemporary Jesuit social justice apostolate. Many phrases and components of

---

9. Ronald Modras, *Ignatian Humanism: A Dynamic Spirituality for the 21st Century* (Chicago: Loyola Press, 2004), 246.

10. Pedro Miguel Lamet, *Pedro Arrupe: Witness of the Twentieth Century, Prophet of the Twenty-First* (Boston College: Institute of Jesuit Sources, 2020). On pages 38–43 Lamet gives a powerful description of these two experiences and how they helped shape Arrupe's perspective on social justice. Lamet uses the translation of "yam" for what the boy is holding, while Modras uses "roll." I have elected to use Modras's translation here.

Jesuit justice initiatives draw on this speech for inspiration. However, we shouldn't dismiss the importance of small chance encounters, some of which undoubtedly contributed to the ideas behind Arrupe's speech. It is the same for each of us. In fact, the nascent experiences of injustice within all people are seeds that can later bear fruit. In some cases, people realize in the moment that the injustice before them is an opportunity to enact the Gospel imperative of service. Other times, it is not until later that the person uncovers the working of the Holy Spirit, despite knowing the reality of the evil of injustice.

Pedro Arrupe's encounter with the boy eating bread and the widows and children were moments of vision, moments when the reality of hunger and subjugation became tangible faces that were logged in his memory. Perhaps he knew then that those moments would be frozen in time on his heart, or maybe it was not until years later when he was elected superior general and had to plot a course for the Society that those faces emerged from his narrative. In either case, the Spirit broke through the random encounters of one individual with another to foster the love of God in tenderness and vulnerability. Perhaps the Society of Jesus owes its current work in social justice to a small, fatherless boy eating a piece of bread on the streets of Madrid. Maybe it was the moment when the young medical student, setting his sights on a worldly career, could say, "I was blind . . . and now I see." A moment of metanoia. The boy was not denied bread by God to teach Arrupe, but rather, in this encounter, the work of God was made visible.

Boy-with-Bread Moments

In my work with the Jesuit Volunteer Corps, *Rostro de Cristo*, and the Ignatian Solidarity Network, I often challenge retreatants or volunteers to reflect on this story of Pedro Arrupe and to look at their own narratives that brought them to working for justice. I refer to this as a "boy-with-bread moment." Using the lessons of *The Spirituality of Imperfection*, I acknowledge that this excavation into their memory may produce results that they wish to forget. During the exercise I invite them to publicly share as little or as much of the story as they choose; however, I encourage them to at least share the complete story with their own heart and with God. Over the years, people have asked, "What if I do not have such an experience?" While I think that is certainly possible and I would never pressure someone to fabricate one, in most cases people have not taken the time to ask themselves how they came upon the desire to work for justice. If a young woman or man is willing to volunteer for a cause, especially for two years of her or his life, there is almost certainly a moment, conversation, or illumination that planted that seed.

It is also important to realize that these experiences do not have to come from performing service in the community. Some of the participants share stories from their own homes and within their families. There is no objective standard to measure an awakening moment that calls someone to the realization of injustice and the need to transform our world. Marginalization or discrimination does not have to be something observed. It can just as easily be something personally experienced.

In the same way that I ask retreatants and volunteers to explore their memory for a boy-with-bread moment, I would like to ask you to do so as part one concludes. It could be something impersonal, like seeing something on the news as a child or overhearing a comment in school. Or, it could be a personal encounter, like Arrupe's experiences. It can take time to sift through your memory to find these moments. As you proceed, be gentle. Sifting through the unknown can bring about realizations that you had suppressed or pushed aside that will now bubble to the surface. It may be helpful to talk to people who care about you as you undergo this self-examination. Indeed, the sharing of these stories in the context of orientations and retreats often leads to conversations that continue late into the evening. I would like to reflect upon a few of the experiences I have had in the context of accompaniment as people sifted through their memories to discern their boy-with-bread moments.

I am astonished by the stories people share during these sessions and the burdens that they carry which resulted from these encounters. One of the most common realizations is captured in the words, "And she was a person too." It seems so obvious, and yet, the denial of personhood is one of the ways people are often marginalized. The Spirit breaking through to illuminate the fragile personhood of another is often the first moment of new vision. A high school student once used the phrase "stares that shattered my soul." This insight is so applicable to vision and powerful in its articulation. As one person looks at another and truly sees the other for the gift of God that they embody, the look goes beyond the eyes and into the soul. While I rarely take notes on the specifics of the stories that are shared, I usually write down a phrase that stands out, from what I perceive as the moment of metanoia. Sometimes rereading these phrases forms a closing prayer. Some examples over the years are: "holding him revealed the importance of presence"; "the sensation of hunger, I wouldn't wish that on anyone"; "he gave the biggest hugs, she gave the biggest smiles—this isn't right, she was living this way"; "she had HIV and likely wouldn't get adopted"; "I could feel her heart beating against mine"; "he struggled with the proper way to ask and I struggled with the proper way to listen"; "my heart breaks and I have a lot of trouble seeing how God is going to fill in those cracks"; "his backpack had ripped and he was terrified to go home"; "she made the Sign of the Cross and grabbed my hand."

I would like to share one story in its entirety because it did not involve a stranger or another country. It was shared by a high school student living in New York City. While others shared about working in soup kitchens or sitting with the elderly, this young man's story began with him playing with his friends on a random afternoon. Then, he returned home for the evening. I was unsure where the story was going, but his voice began to quiver and everyone in the circle turned toward him. "It was later that night when my friend called," he said as his voice cracked. "'Can my family come to stay with you? Our apartment flooded . . . we lost everything we owned.'" The young man telling the story began to cry, and the vulnerability of his best friend in making the call became his vulnerability in sharing the story. It wasn't a stranger who revealed to him the fragility of the human condition. It was someone just like him who had suffered the effects of the environment and the New York City floods. The storyteller said his friend's family stayed with them for a few weeks. He never looked at his home and possessions in the same way. He saw things differently and enacted the charity of the Gospel by offering shelter to his friends. Metanoia moved him to the *magna anima*.

When I ask volunteers or retreatants to share their boy-with-bread experiences, I feel obliged to share my own. It is at that time that I share with them the story of my first service experience on the streets of Cleveland. How I, like Arrupe, grew up in a middle-class family and had little experience of poverty. I never had to worry about where my next meal would come from and rarely thought about those who did. Places with "poor people" were "bad areas of town" that my family would avoid when driving through the city. I do not think my parents are bad people. I think that when I was growing up they prioritized what they saw as "safety" over exposure to different cultures, races, or socio-economic backgrounds. It is in this context that I existed prior to my boy-with-bread moment. We all have experiences and backgrounds that are important to recognize, because they play a seminal role in the way we interpret boy-with-bread moments. Perhaps my experience would be entitled "man with hot dogs." Like Arrupe, it was my first real encounter with poverty in the space where those who are oppressed by systemic injustice reside. And I, like Arrupe, will not forget the first time I saw things in a new way, where the small soul of self-centeredness inched toward the *imago Dei*.

Reflection Questions

1. Spend time reflecting on your own narrative. Do you have a boy-with-bread moment? Again, this does not have to be a long story. It can be something you overheard or a random encounter. If you feel comfortable, share the story with someone who can help you unpack the ways it has helped shape your narrative and your desire to serve.

2. As you reflect on the narratives where you saw issues of justice differently, also take time to examine your own background and upbringing. How might these factors have influenced your boy-with-bread encounter?

Conclusion

Your Principle, Your Foundation

The title of part one, "The Principle and the Foundation," is inspired by the twenty-third annotation of the *Spiritual Exercises* of St. Ignatius, which is referred to as "the Principle and Foundation." My friend and mentor, Paula Fitzgerald, often refers to this annotation as St. Ignatius's mission statement. In it, Ignatius affirms God as creator, the importance of the gifts God gives to human beings, and God's desire for us to use these gifts to grow in relationship with God. On the final day of the Manresa retreat at John Carroll, Paula would invite the retreatants to write their own mission statement, in light of having spent the retreat reflecting on Ignatius's Principle and Foundation. Like Ignatius, they spent time reflecting on their lives, determining their non-negotiables, and staking a claim to a small part of themselves.

In some ways, part one has invited you to do the same thing to address the first question of the preface. What does it mean to say *you* are called to enter the reality of another? If you are discerning a call to service, what is your mission statement? At this point it isn't about choosing a large or small program, going domestic or international. It isn't about going for a spring break trip or a summer abroad. For now, it is about your story.

I often tell young people who are considering marriage that we see many unsuccessful marriages because people place more of a focus on the "do" instead of the "I" of their marriage vows. Put another way, we are comfortable thinking through and discussing with our partner concepts like jobs, financial priorities, and living location. We are also trained to look for qualities in other people that we find desirable. Scrolling through any dating app will demonstrate what people are looking for in a partner.

Similarly, reviewing different immersion trips based on their locations on a school website or skimming postgraduate volunteer pamphlets only yields limited information. These are all important issues. But the first priority, the first duty, is to discover yourself. Only then can you know what you can offer to another person, a program, or an experience. Finding a service program or discerning a time of service is similar to seeking a relationship. So, spend time with yourself, despite your imperfections. Sift through your memory and your non-negotiables. Tread gently and respect your discoveries, those boy-with-bread moments of metanoic transformation. In the next part we will move to discernment. For now, rest in your journey of exploration before the God of love and mystery. In that place, you will begin to discover your principles and the foundation upon which they rest.

Part Two

Freedom and the Shining Gem

An elderly nun (different from the woman mentioned in the introduction) who had served the church for many years spoke with Father Gray about her spiritual journey. He suggested that she draw images in her journal representing what was in her heart. He also asked her to paperclip the pages together as she went so she would not look back at what she had drawn the previous day. He was hoping the Spirit would guide her to draw images without trying to conform to an expectation or "make sense" of what came previously. Eventually they paged through the images together. When he looked up, he saw tears rolling down her cheeks. The insights from her prayer were not what she expected.

Part one focused on your narrative. You were invited to use imagination and memory to delve deeply and gently into your formative moments of social justice awareness. These are boy-with-bread moments and conversations that have helped form your non-negotiables. I stated that as people of faith we trust that God is there in some way, working to reveal God's self in those encounters. Digging

deeper into God's communication with you will be the sub-
stance of part two. If part one was the stone, the material
of your experience, part two will invite you to chisel away
to uncover the form beneath the stone. What might God
be saying to you during your process of reflection? Chapter
four will begin the process of discernment by exploring God's love using Luke 15's story of the prodigal son.
Chapter five will examine the power of silence in prayer
and in the life of Pedro Arrupe during his time in a prison
in Japan. Finally, chapter six will introduce the Examen,
a form of Ignatian prayer, as a tool for your discernment.
This final chapter of part two will begin the transition from
inner reflection toward an integration of these realizations
in the world that will be the central analysis of the subsequent parts of the book.

Chapter 4

God's Love

I previously mentioned my cousin, Stacie, who did not think she belonged at Mass on Christmas Eve. She didn't think God wanted her there. The opposite side of the question is to ask why we should believe God *does* want her there. Or, to put it another way, why should we trust that God loves us, despite our sins and shortcomings? The foundational starting point to discernment in the Christian tradition is a relationship in which we believe, as a matter of faith, that God will guide us to a place of Truth. This cornerstone of the Christian faith, that God desires what is truly best and most life-giving for human creatures, is part of what motivates us to reach out to God for guidance.

A few years ago at the Jesuit Volunteer Corps and *Rostro de Cristo* orientation I was giving a presentation on Ignatian spirituality. I discussed the way St. Ignatius wrote in his *Autobiography* that God "treated him as a schoolmaster treats a child he is teaching."[11] I paused at this point

---

11. Ignatius of Loyola, "The Autobiography," in *Ignatius of Loyola: The Spiritual Exercises and Selected Works*, ed. George Ganss, S.J. (New York: Paulist Press, 1991), 79.

to reaffirm for the volunteers the truth that Ignatius was articulating in that memory: God's love. The metaphor of a schoolmaster guiding a pupil is how Ignatius felt about God guiding him during his experience in the small town of Manresa. Still a neophyte in matters of faith, Ignatius was being gently nudged by the God of love to grow closer to God, even while he did not understand exactly how. When we took a break, I was approached by a volunteer named Dom. This was only the second day of the two-week formation program, so I had not yet met Dom, but I could tell he was unsettled and was holding back tears. "Thank you," he said. "I have always been told that God loves me, but something about the way you said it in that moment hit me and made me believe it in a new way." I deflected credit and mused that it was not about the way I said it, but the Spirit working in that moment who gave him this new insight. Dom experienced a moment similar to Thomas Merton at Fourth and Walnut (mentioned in part one). Each saw himself shining like the sun, basking in the love of God.

One Scripture passage that powerfully speaks to the love of God is chapter 15 of Luke's Gospel. At the start of the chapter Jesus is speaking with sinners and tax collectors. The Pharisees are dismayed that he would spend time with "those people" and in reply Jesus offers three parables. The first is about a shepherd who had ninety-nine sheep, but leaves them to search for one lost sheep. The second parable is about a woman who searches for a lost coin. When she finds it, although she has nine others, she rejoices. In both cases, the actions seem counter-intuitive.

Why endanger ninety-nine sheep for one? Why look for one coin when you have others? However, Jesus is affirming the importance of each sheep, each coin.

The third parable is about a prodigal son. There are a number of culturally relevant details in the narrative that need to be considered in order to understand the way Jesus' audience would have interpreted it. The story begins with a son who demands his inheritance from his father while he is still alive. Culturally, such an action was akin to saying, "Father, I wish you were dead." Yet, the father acquiesces and gives the young son his inheritance. The youth departs and spends the money frivolously. In his lowest point, sitting in pig filth, he has a metanoia moment and sees things in a new way. He decides to go back to his father to beg for a role as a servant in his house. The text says that while the youth was a long way off, the father saw his son, was filled with compassion, and ran to him. First, to see him from a long way off makes it sound as though the father was actively looking for him. Moreover, in the ancient world an elder would not usually run, especially to greet someone younger.

These actions of the father do not seem very strange to contemporary audiences. Sure, it seems odd, but isn't impossible. But for Jesus' audience, this sequence of events was much more improbable. I imagine his listeners scoffing at the foolishness of the father. Yet, Jesus is teaching us about the love of God, not merely about the forgiveness of a fictional father who loves his son unconditionally. In conjunction with the previous two parables and the initial challenge to Jesus about eating with sinners and tax collectors, the parable takes on a more powerful meaning: This is the love of God for us all.

As mentioned in part one, rereading a story or revisiting your own story at different points in your life can alter the way you hear and interpret the message. For some of my friends who have difficult relationships with their fathers, this passage is not very helpful. They have not experienced the love of a father to use as a good analogy. This is a pitfall of the use of any story that is trying to articulate a truth through metaphor. While keeping this in mind, I offer the parables of Luke 15 as a Gospel affirmation of the truth that Dom came to realize. God does love us. As we move forward to apply some tools for uncovering the way God is working through our stories, I ask you to keep this insight as the platform upon which your discoveries rest.

Discernment

Once we trust that God is a loving God, we can move to discernment, one of the key buzzwords in the Ignatian lexicon. Discernment is ultimately about choosing between two goods. This is one key difference between decision-making and discernment. One can make a decision about what to eat for dinner or what to wear to a party. That is not discernment. Discernment involves prayer, reflection, conversation, and the realization that while any option can lead to a good outcome, there may be one option that leads to a greater good. Likely, many readers who are considering short-term immersion or long-term service options are undergoing discernment. When introducing discernment in a college classroom, I invite my students to think about whether they underwent discernment when picking a college, deciding on a major, or considering graduate schools.

The archetype for Ignatian discernment is the near-death experience of St. Ignatius. Having been wounded at Pamplona, young Inigo, as he was known at that time, lay in bed recovering. He wanted to be a great soldier and imagined a life of knightly combat. But his desires were also informed by his reading materials, stories on the saints and the life of Christ. Over a period of time, he noticed that these daydreams caused different internal outcomes. When he thought about being a knight of the world, he would feel excitement at first, but empty later. However, when reflecting on serving as a "knight" for Christ, as the saints did, he felt both initial and enduring excitement. Ultimately, upon his recovery, Inigo chose the life that was closer to his "knight for Christ" ambitions. These are two good things—a knight who protects his kingdom and a knight who "protects" Christ. Inigo was not choosing between good and evil, but between two goods. The stirrings in his heart moved him to the greater good.

Although Ignatius wasn't aware that he was engaging in discernment during this time, in his later years he looked back at his life and was able to name that experience. Similar to the exercise in part one where you were asked to look back at your life, Ignatius was invited to do so in dictating what became his autobiography. Although he hesitated, he was nudged by other Jesuits who wanted a written record for younger and future Jesuits who would not be able to get to know Ignatius personally. This experience in his life also played a role in creating the text of the *Spiritual Exercises*. This document, written near the end of Ignatius's life, is a guidebook for the person who gives the Exercises to a retreatant. It is here that Ignatius spells out important definitions for discernment, consolation, and desolation.

Within the *Spiritual Exercises*, St. Ignatius includes a section entitled "Rules for the Discernment of Spirits." In the first annotation of this section, he explains that these are rules "to aid us towards perceiving and then understanding . . . the various motions which are caused in the soul."[12] When one is discerning between two good choices, it is possible to be drawn to a good choice for the wrong reasons. For example, wanting to participate in an immersion program (usually a good thing) because you want to go on multiple trips to win an award at graduation (a problematic motivation). Or, one may choose to do a year of service because an outside voice, such as a parent or teacher, is unduly influencing you. The desire to do postgraduate volunteer work can also be a form of rebellion against parents who seem overly protective. In these cases, the end goal of service is likely good, but the way one reaches that goal can be due to what Ignatius called "inordinate attachments." Our intentions should be

---

12. Ignatius, "The Spiritual Exercises," in *Spiritual Exercises*, [313]. Quotations from the Exercises are cited by annotation instead of page number, and the annotation number is placed in brackets.

directed toward what can lead us close to God, not toward attachments like fame, power, or independence.

Thus, discerning should be undertaken by looking at how one's internal motivations lead toward consolation and desolation. There are many components of consolation, but for our purposes, it can be understood with Ignatius's definition, as "every increase in hope, faith, and charity, and every interior joy which calls and attracts one towards heavenly things."[13] Meanwhile, desolation can be understood as "darkness of soul, turmoil within it, an impulsive motion towards low and earthly things, or disquiet from various agitations and temptations."[14] So, in our previous examples, glory for doing immersion work or rebellion by doing a year of volunteer service are "impulsive motions towards low and earthly things." These motivations do not point to heavenly things that give glory to God. Rather, they give glory to us. A person who is truly discerning service work should take the time to process their motivations.

In light of these terms, I hope you can return to those boy-with-bread moments of your past anew. Within those stories, are there examples of consolation or desolation? In what ways might God have been speaking to you at that time and how do you interpret those recollections now? Looking ahead, as Ignatius did during his recovery, begin to think about the possible realities that you are discerning now. Perhaps you are thinking about traveling for a short-term immersion but are worried about safety or

---

13. Ignatius, "The Spiritual Exercises," [316].
14. Ignatius, "The Spiritual Exercises," [317].

group dynamics. Maybe you are weighing a service program for a year but are not sure if you want to remain in the United States or travel abroad. Perhaps graduate school or a relationship is weighing on your discernment as well. Reflect on the possibilities in your prayer. Envision yourself moving forward with each one. What questions rise to the surface during prayer? Journal about those inquiries. Bring these reflections to people who care about you and who know you best. These are all components of discernment.

There are two images I like to use when explaining discernment to students. The first is mining for gold. When miners look for gold, they use a device that sorts out the soot and stones from the gold by spinning it quickly and then straining out the excess. The gold is there from the beginning; it is just obscured by other material. In this way, your deepest desires are within you. You are inviting God to remove some of the excess soot (inordinate attachments) to clear the way for your vision. In Ignatian terms, an inordinate attachment is anything that distracts us from our deepest desires.

My second image is of a sailboat on the water with the sails up to catch the wind, but with no device to steer. The boat can go where the wind takes it, without preconceived preparation. This, too, is discernment. The Spirit could take you places you never expect. Try not to put limitations on your discernment. A student may think she is discerning between majoring in business or in English and end up becoming an education major after a year. Or a person may be torn between domestic and international one-year service programs, only to end up doing two years of service with a previously unknown program. Discernment is ultimately about the freedom to respond to the call of our loving God, which is not something imposed from the outside, but shining like a gem inside us all along.

Reflection Questions

1. In what ways have you experienced God's love for you, specifically? Like Dom, do you sometimes struggle with accepting that God loves you? Spend time in prayer sharing with God your gratitude, your doubts, and everything in between.

2. Why do you want to engage in service work? Spend time in prayer, inviting God into that decision. Do this over a period of time, not just once. Take time to notice your feelings and emotions during your prayer. What brings you consolation and what causes you desolation?

Chapter 5

Silence

I love music. There is nothing like listening to my favorite band, Mumford and Sons, while sitting with my eyes closed or while grading papers. So, when the radio went out in my car when I first started driving (yes, before smartphones!) it was a long forty-five-minute drive across town to have the radio fixed. Driving with no sound was quite the experience for a seventeen-year-old! We are so accustomed to sound that not having music or noise can be irritating or scary for many people. Discernment requires silence. The opening story of part two involved an elderly nun examining her life. In telling this story to our class, Father Gray relayed the importance of silence in her experience, as well as the role of silence in their personal discussions. Although she was not initially able to articulate what was going on in her soul, the nun was able to draw images once she removed the external noise from her life. Those images eventually revealed something within her that she did not expect.

For many people, their lifestyle is full of noise. Noise can be auditory or psychological and mental. By this, I mean something that draws one away from a primary task or focus. A few years ago I walked into a friend's apartment. He was in his bedroom, but the television was on in another room. When I asked him why his TV was on even though he wasn't watching it, he replied that he "needed the noise." Noise can also be the constant need to be connected to a cell phone, even when the volume is low or muted. Between various apps or texting, people are easily distracted from whatever they are doing or the person they are with at the moment. If you are waiting to get your oil changed, sitting at a doctor's office, or waiting for a bus, notice how many people are looking down at their phone or other device. The idea of silence is very counter-cultural. Perhaps an environment of silence is needed now, more than ever before.

As I have indicated, cultivating an atmosphere of silence does not only include the reduction of auditory sounds. In part one I mentioned the *Spiritual Exercises* of St. Ignatius while discussing the First Principle and Foundation. The retreat experience of the Exercises requires an atmosphere of silence in order to listen to the movements within one's heart. Ignatius believed that blocking out the noise of life, both the noise found in the world and the noise found in the competing and complex desires within oneself, can allow a person to more clearly discern God's call. Perhaps a good analogy is the experience of having static or interference while listening to a radio or watching television during a storm. The sounds can seem distant or garbled, which makes the message difficult to decipher. The sound becomes sharper as the interference subsides. As external noise is eliminated, the sound of God's call becomes clearer.

One of my roles at the *Rostro de Cristo* and Jesuit Volunteer International orientation was to prepare the volunteers for their three-day retreat and to have spiritual conversations with them during it. Because the volunteers had usually been together for a week prior to the retreat, they had become friends and found it difficult to stop talking to one another for three days. In order to drive home the importance of silence and solitude, I challenged them to not even acknowledge one another's presence with a nod or smile. For readers who have been on an Ignatian silent retreat, this rule may seem draconian. However, I explained that you never know if the other person is in a deep and reflective space. A smile or nod could lead to laughter, which could pull the other person away from a powerful insight. While this is a stringent interpretation of the silence of an Ignatian retreat, the volunteers often appreciated this approach by the end because it allowed them the freedom to focus on themselves and their prayer, rather than the typical social formalities of greeting people.

Silence is not only a gift during a retreat. When Father Gray moved to Washington, DC, to take a position at Georgetown University, I endeavored to visit him at least once a year. I saw it as a spiritual pilgrimage. One evening while I was staying at the Georgetown Jesuit residence, Father Gray and I returned from dinner and watched a movie in his room. At the end of the movie, I looked over and saw his eyes were closed. It wasn't unusual for him to fall asleep like this, being a man in his eighties. I decided to sit in the rocking chair across from him and close my eyes for a few moments as well. After a short time, I heard him say,

"Isn't it nice, Jimmy, that we are the kind of friends who can sit in silence together? I love you, Jimmy." I became choked up and couldn't immediately respond. Eventually the weight of his beautiful statement settled in my heart and I simply responded, "I love you too, Abba [my nickname for him]."

Since that time, I have noticed silent moments with other friends for whom I care deeply. In some cases, I share my memory of Father Gray's wisdom and am reminded once again of the beauty of silence. Hopefully, there are a few friends in your life with whom you can sit in silence, not needing to fill the void with noise. Just the authenticity of two human beings basking in the love of God. In part four we will again return to the power of silence, but as a tool to bring presence to one who is suffering. The rest of this chapter will examine the power of silence for Arrupe and a time he was able to transform this silence into love.

Confinement and Freedom

In December 1941, Pedro Arrupe was arrested by the Japanese authorities on suspicion of being a spy for the Allied powers. Although he had lived in Japan for three years, the outbreak of hostilities between Japan and the United States in World War II made him a suspect. While under arrest, Arrupe's time was spent either alone in the quiet of a cell, or under interrogation from the *Kempeitai*, the Japanese military police, who thought he would break and admit his guilt. At times the guards would come to speak with him about his religion, and Arrupe enjoyed preaching to them about God. These friendships remained once Arrupe was released from jail. During interrogations, Arrupe often told his life story, how he was a doctor and became a priest after witnessing miracles at Lourdes. While interesting to his interrogators, these stories could in no way prove his innocence. The letters that had been taken from Arrupe's home seemed to be the evidence the Japanese needed to put him to death for crimes against Japan.

On Christmas evening Arrupe especially yearned to say Mass, but his captors would not allow him this opportunity. As he sat miserable in his cell, he heard voices from outside. Arrupe explains:

> Suddenly, above the murmur that was reaching me, there arose a soft, sweet, consoling Christmas carol, one of the songs which I had myself taught to my Christians. They were my Christians who, heedless of the danger of being themselves imprisoned, had come to console me, to console their Shimpu Sama (their priest), who was away that Christmas night which hitherto we had always celebrated with great joy. What a contrast between that thoughtfulness and the injustice of senseless imprisonment![15]

---

15. Pedro Arrupe, S.J., "The Eucharist and Youth," in *Other Apostolates Today*, ed. Jerome Aixala, S.J. (St. Louis, MO: The Institute of Jesuit Sources, 1981), 299–300.

This experience brought him a new understanding of the comfort of Christ and encouraged him at one of the lowest times in his confinement. Arrupe explained, "I felt that [Jesus] also descended into my heart, and that night I made the best spiritual Communion of all my life."[16] The consolation received amidst his desolation, loneliness, and fear allowed Arrupe to totally give himself over to Christ. In that time of mutual donation, Arrupe felt Christ's love abundantly in his heart; this experience of communion brought him consolation. These moments of silence in his cell became opportunities of deep prayer during his confinement.

At midnight on January 11, 1942, Arrupe's cell was thrown open as the guards burst in and escorted him out. He feared that it was for his execution. What followed instead were thirty-seven hours of continuous interrogation, where he was questioned about politics, religion, and numerous "inconsistencies" in his beliefs. After this interrogation he was escorted back to his cell. But only a half hour later his door opened again. This time he was escorted to the prison governor's office and, to his surprise and delight, was informed that he was being released. He was told that he had been imprisoned because of rumors against him, but that the Japanese believed "one of the best ways of judging the innocence or guilt of the accused is to examine him closely in his everyday actions."[17] Such observations reveal the inner person and the character within

---

16. Arrupe, "The Eucharist and Youth," 299-300.
17. George D. Bishop, *Pedro Arrupe, S.J.: Twenty-Eighth General of the Society of Jesus* (Anand, Gujarat, India: Gujarat Sahitya Prakash, 2000), 75.

one's inner being. It was not his theological arguments that had saved his life, but rather "his internal completeness, his simplicity, his transparency of soul."[18]

Before leaving the prison, Arrupe wished to thank each of the guards who watched over him. To their astonishment, this man who had been falsely imprisoned and isolated for over a month was thanking them for the experience. Arrupe then told the head of the prison that he wished to thank him as well. Shocked, the governor asked him to explain. Arrupe replied, "Yes. You have taught me to suffer. I came to Japan to suffer for the Japanese people. For a Christian to suffer is not a matter of pain or strain. Jesus Christ suffered more than any other man. The believer is not afraid to suffer with or like Christ. You have helped me to understand this."[19] The governor fought back tears and told Arrupe he was free to preach his religion.

After the war, the United States war crimes investigators asked Father Arrupe for the names of those who had held him captive, but he refused to give them. He did not want revenge on those who had done him wrong, but wanted to move forward to forgiveness and healing.[20] Just as the resurrection narratives tell how the resurrected Christ offered consolation to the disciples, rather than revenge on his persecutors, Arrupe returned to his cell one last time devoid of the desire for revenge, but filled with the hope of consolation.

---

18. Bishop, *Pedro Arrupe*, 76.
19. Bishop, *Pedro Arrupe*, 76.
20. Bishop, *Pedro Arrupe*, 77.

Arrupe later reflected that despite his suffering, it was an instructive thirty-three days. He observed, "How much I learned then! I believe that it was the month in which I learned the most in my life. Alone as I was, I learned the knowledge of silence, of loneliness, of harsh and severe poverty, the interior conversation with 'the guest of my soul' who had never shown himself to be more 'sweet' than then."[21] Arrupe also learned what it means to be powerless and how much loving deeds can mean to someone who is alone when his young Christians came to sing to him.[22]

Although a month of isolation is not the goal of an immersive service experience, Arrupe's experiences with silence can be instructive for us all. In order to sift for gold, or to chisel the stone of our lives, we need the right tools. Silence can become the sifter that helps us remove inordinate attachments, which are aspects that cloud our vision of God's call. Stepping away from the noise of the world can reveal internal workings of the heart that are otherwise obscured by the noise around us. During your time of discernment it is crucial to spend time in prayer and silence, listening to the pull of your heart, trusting in the love of God. This God is the shepherd who will not leave a single sheep to the wolves and who will spend an eternity searching for the one lost coin. This God is the loving God who will call the angel choirs to sing to your heart as you dig deeper for the shining gem.

---

21. Arrupe, "The Eucharist and Youth," 298–299.
22. Hedwig Lewis, S.J., *Pedro Arrupe Treasury* (Gujarat, India: Gujarat Sahitya Prakask, 2007), 31.

Reflection Questions

1. Make a list of the friends and family members whom you can sit in silence with without pretense or discomfort. What makes these relationships so special?

2. Have you had an experience like Arrupe's where you have used silence to transform a difficult decision or circumstance into a place of God's love? How might this experience help to inform the way you approach your immersive service experience?

Chapter 6

The Examen

Another one of my roles with the Jesuit Volunteers and *Rostro de Cristo* has been leading the volunteers through the Ignatian Examen each night of orientation. The Examen is a form of prayer utilized by St. Ignatius that is rooted in the *Spiritual Exercises*. Although Ignatius did not invent the concept of examining one's conscience for movements of the Spirit, he shifted the emphasis away from sin, which was previously the central issue.[23] In my role I would explain on the first night that the Examen is about identifying the rhythm and relationship during the prayer experience. In other words, looking for the rhythm of one's life within one's relationship with God. While reflecting upon the day through the steps of the prayer, what rises to the surface that may have previously been unseen? In light of these realizations, what might that mean for growing in relationship with God?

For those preparing for one or two years of international service, praying the Examen each evening was meant to create a space for vulnerability and openness. The major-

---

23. James Martin, S.J., *Learning to Pray: A Guide for Everyone* (New York: Harper One, 2021), 138.

ity of the volunteers left for their new homes immediately following orientation, while some waited approximately six months before leaving the country. For those whose departure was imminent, the Examen could help them be honest with themselves and with God about their fears and anxiety. Those waiting the additional months were invited to continue praying the Examen as preparation for the journey and balancing having one foot raised to the future while physically waiting in the United States. In both cases, we hoped that this form of prayer could be woven into their experience as a volunteer, offering them a helpful tool and a way of asking how God is present during their day.

There are numerous ways of praying the Examen. After offering a formulaic approach for the sake of learning the Examen during the first few evenings of orientation, I would encourage the volunteers to make the experience their own. The same is true for you as you are discerning volunteer and service experiences. Therefore, the following comments should be viewed as an introduction to what the Examen is trying to accomplish, while leaving open the myriad possible approaches to this goal. As with many of the exercises in this text, it is invitational, not restrictive. I encourage you to research online how different organizations have adapted the Examen to their context.

One helpful text on the Examen is *The Examen Prayer: Ignatian Wisdom for Our Lives Today* by Timothy Gallagher, OVM. Gallagher breaks the components of the Examen into five movements or prayer periods: gratitude, petition, review, forgiveness, and renewal.[24] I used these five movements during the orientation program. On the first evening I would spend roughly three minutes on each step, but would elongate the review step by a few minutes. On each subsequent evening I would increase the overall prayer time. During the second week of orientation the volunteers could leave the chapel and complete the Examen on their own if they felt they did not need my verbal promptings and questions to spur their reflection.

Before beginning the Examen, as with many forms of prayer, finding a quiet place to center your mind and quiet your heart is important. Posture is also important. While it is good to be comfortable, you do not want to be so comfortable that your body thinks it is time to sleep. Occasionally the volunteers, who were putting in twelve-hour days of discussion and reflection, would need to be reminded of this point! As you settle into a prayerful position, focus on your breathing and the slowing of your heartbeat as you enter into prayer. The first step for Gallagher is gratitude. Begin by noticing the gifts of God from the day. What is it that I am grateful for at this moment of prayer? Perhaps a conversation with a friend, an experience in prayer, a good meal, or a special moment is what you are most thankful for at this time. Ignatius challenges us to see how all of these things lead back to God and can create a foundation of gratitude in our lives.

---

24. Timothy Gallagher, OVM, *The Examen Prayer: Ignatian Wisdom for Our Lives Today* (New York: Crossroad Publishing, 2006), 25.

The second step is petition. What am I asking of God in this moment? For the volunteers this sometimes took the form of strength, consolation for their decision to undergo a lengthy service commitment, or support for loved ones whom they may not see for two years. The third step, review, can be the lengthiest of the five steps. Here, one reflects on the experiences of the day and perhaps how one has experienced God's presence. Gallagher explains, "I look for the stirrings in my heart and the thoughts that God has given me. . . . I also look for those that have not been of God."[25] When leading the group through this point I would try to hit upon common touch points that I knew we all experienced, and then invite them to fill in the gaps. For example, I knew we all had meals at the same time, so I nudged them to think back to the conversations at their tables. I knew we attended the same sessions and would ask how they felt during the discussions, such as those on appropriate power dynamics or healthy relationships. Ignatius is not only asking us to review the events of our day, but to go deeper and examine the internal movements in our heart at different moments.

The fourth step is forgiveness. How might God be present and offer a healing touch where I was most out of step with God's love? We are not perfect. We sometimes fall short of being the women and men God calls us to be. Coming to terms with these areas for growth can help us move toward reconciliation, whether that be with others, with ourselves,

---

25. Gallagher, *The Examen*, 25.

or with God. And finally, the renewal during the fifth step looks for the ways that these insights might be applied to the following day. In light of these realizations, how can I move into tomorrow more in tune to God's role in my life? How can I treat others with more respect and love?

Another helpful guide to the Examen is Jim Manney's book *A Simple Life-Changing Prayer: Discovering the Power of St. Ignatius Loyola's Examen.* He offers a similar breakdown in praying the Examen, with a few minor differences. Manney modifies the first step to be "ask for light" and instructs that we begin by praying for a kind of grace where "we want to see our everyday life through God's eyes."[26] This grace is to know ourselves and to know what we really want in life. Manney reminds us that these insights will not come through burning bushes or booming voices, but "in the quiet whisper of our Spirit-guided memories, thoughts, and feelings."[27] Manney's second step, "give thanks," is similar to Gallagher's initial step on gratitude. Again, there are many ways to do the Examen. It is about finding the way that best fits your spirituality.

Jim Martin's book *Learning to Pray: A Guide for Everyone* contains a helpful chapter on the Examen. Martin's five steps are: presence, gratitude, review, sorrow, and grace. In his discussion of the fourth step, Martin remarks on the difference between shame and guilt, two feelings one could have when experiencing sorrow for one's decisions during

---

26. Jim Manney, *A Simple Life-Changing Prayer: Discovering the Power of St. Ignatius Loyola's Examen* (Chicago: Loyola Press, 2001), 25.

27. Manney, *Life-Changing Prayer*, 26.

the day. He points out, "Guilt says, 'I did a bad thing.' Shame says, 'I am a bad person.' Too often guilt, which can be healthy, leads to shame, which can be unhealthy."[28] These are important aspects of your character to explore when discerning service work or reviewing your experiences of becoming aware of social injustices. Similar to part one, when we explored the role of narrative, it is important to be gentle with yourself and the realizations that you have that may involve shame and guilt. Guilt about not taking an action can spur you on to a change in the days ahead, while shame can stop you in your growth and weigh you down. At moments when the Examen becomes heavy it can be helpful to return to the previous chapters or reflections that emphasize God's love. These exercises are not designed to weigh you down with shame for your past. Rather, they should ultimately lead to a stronger relationship with God and a deeper understanding of your internal motivations.

In my own prayer life I have found the Examen to be a helpful exercise for reminding me of the importance of gratitude and the way God is present at times when I am most inclined to forget. A number of years ago I was in a long-distance relationship and my former partner and I were looking for a way to cultivate a deeper spiritual connection. We began jointly praying the Examen in the evenings, which helped us go deeper in our reflections. Beginning our prayer with gratitude and ending with renewal helped us articulate the important and life-giving aspects of our

---

28. Martin, *Learning to Pray* 149.

day with the promise to carry them forward to the next day. She often challenged me to grow in my relationship with God while continuing to grow in our relationship together. The Examen does not have to be individual. I encourage you to be creative with this style of prayer, for example by focusing on art, music, silence, discussion, or any other medium in which you are seeking to be more attuned to the presence of God in the world.

This section on the Examen is far from comprehensive. I invite you to look at the resources mentioned and to explore other opportunities to practice it. The Ignatian Solidarity Network often publishes themed Examens focusing on politics, the environment, and other social justice issues. For the purposes of your current discernment, I hope that you can weave the Examen prayer into your reflections. It is a way to notice how God is working through the rhythm and relationships of your day to reveal God's love in a transformative way. Just as the miner searches for gold by shaking pans to remove dross, you are shaking loose the inordinate attachments that surround the precious longings of your heart. Inviting God into the search can reveal a valuable jewel.

Reflection Question

1. Incorporate the Examen into your daily prayer routine for one week. Journal about your experiences each evening and look for reoccurring themes. How might God be speaking to you through these illuminations?

Conclusion

The Call of the Loving God

Part two began with a story from Father Gray's conversations with an elderly nun and the pictures she drew in her journal. As she and Father Gray reviewed the images she began to weep. The tears were not from joy. They resulted from a realization of deep sadness. The pictures began as small stick figures and each day the image became more complete, culminating in a family of stick figures in front of a home with a garden. Sobbing, the woman explained that during her prayer she realized that she only became a nun because of her difficult relationship with her mother. She often tried to outdo her mother and the one thing that she could do that her mother could not was to become a nun. In this moment, she realized that her life had been dedicated to a pursuit that had always been a cloudy, spurious venture. What would have made her truly happy was the family that she would now never know.

Not taking the time to dig deeply into your call to service can leave you like this disheartened nun, set adrift without an authentic understanding of herself. One can follow through the motions of expectations placed upon us by our parents, friends, or classmates. We could want to do service as a résumé builder or an opportunity for recognition and glory. But ultimately, in order to answer the question established in the preface—What does it mean to be called to service?—it is vital to spend time in the silence of your heart, seeking the will of the loving God.

I think it is appropriate to end part two with an example of how discernment is an ongoing reflection, rather than a singular epiphany. A number of years ago my friend Eric called to ask for advice, as he was discerning a new job. He had been working in healthcare and his wife was in residency for medical school. They had one child with another on the way. He explained to me that for a few years he had had a growing desire to become an assistant pastor at a church. As a non-Catholic, his discernment did not involve joining a seminary and leaving his wife and children. Rather, it centered on the large pay cut that he would be taking at a time when his wife was still completing medical school. He would be putting his family into financial uncertainty at a critical time. However, during his prayer he felt a strong consolation to pursue this new vocation. It was not a passing fancy, but something that recurred in his prayer over a lengthy period. He explained his concern that if this inkling was truly from God, what would it mean if he did not act on it?

Upon hearing his story, I offered that perhaps God *was* calling him to ministry, but added that one can be called to something in the future. Discernment is about the ongoing rhythm and relationship with God. Feeling called to something, such as becoming a pastor, could be a very strong and authentic prayer realization, but the next question for his discernment could focus on *when* he should answer this call. Perhaps he should wait a year or two and continue to pray about the opportunity. His family's needs could mean waiting until his wife completed medical school. Waiting to answer a call does not devalue the results of the initial discernment. Eric ultimately chose to wait, and after roughly one year, accepted a position as an assistant pastor.

Eric's story is a lesson for all of us living in a time of instant gratification. Even if the "gratification" is in answer to a very earnest desire to serve God, it may need to wait. Having a true desire to experience an immersion or postgraduate volunteer program is not the only question. Particularly when the time period is lengthy, other considerations, such as one's need to be present to an elderly family member or sick friend, should be taken into account. The discernment is not only between you and God, but the "you" that is bound together in the fabric of life. Engaging in a service experience, no matter how long, is a privilege, not an obligation. Do not forget to include the needs of others in your life in your reflection. I am not saying that God could never call a person to make the choice to eschew other obligations. Nor am I saying that God would never call a person to service if that person has a sick family member. There will always be reasons to not act if you want to find them. I am simply offering that the search for God's call should include the freedom of exploring multiple dimensions of the question. A proper discernment should try to consider every possible element of the question and should bring all of those known elements to prayer. Perhaps the results of your discernment will be like Eric's, leading you to an authentic desire to serve, but with the caveat of "not yet."

Part two is called "Freedom and the Shining Gem," a reference to the jewel within each of us and our freedom to share that jewel with the world. Father Gray often said that freedom and love are the heart of the Christian message. The love of God described in Luke 15 should be the basis for discernment about how and when to live a life of immersive service. But these questions are not easy, nor automatic. Feeling called to serve radically, to live the Gospel in this way, should not be taken for granted.

While parts one and two have focused on you and your motivations, the next three parts will challenge you to see those whom you will encounter during these experiences as made in the image and likeness of God as well. We are all called to share Christ's love in the world. The question is how your gifts and talents best call you to answer this Gospel imperative. Before moving on, take time to bask in the love of God and remind yourself that you are a shining jewel, called by God, both in the silence of your heart and the cacophony of life.

Part Three

Volunteerism, Voluntourism, and the Savior Complex

Behind me I heard a voice enthusiastically instructing: "A bit to the left. Now, hold that umbrella a bit more to the side. We want to catch the light coming off the train station." When I turned around, I saw a photographer and a woman in an elegant dress holding an umbrella at a forty-five-degree angle. The sun was glancing off the top of the umbrella to create the perfect shade to accentuate her facial features. It was clear that the woman was the central focus of the photograph. Given the position of the camera and the photographer's suggestions, I could tell the backdrop played only a minor role in creating the ambience. Perhaps she is a model or they were creating an advertisement for a product she is wearing, I thought.

Photos help us remember people and places. They can call to mind the past, given that a photo is a concretized image of a previous moment. With the rise of social media, images have also become status symbols or attention-grabbing artifacts that boast of accomplishments and places visited. An accumulation of "likes" can become competitive among friends and can be used to measure the "worth" of one person against another. This can be especially tempting when people travel to new places. Unfortunately, immersions and service opportunities lend themselves to the exploitation of people through the taking and distributing of photos. Usually, the posting of immersion pictures to social media sites isn't done with malicious intent. However, the question of which photographs should or should not be taken is one that offers a gateway into the bigger picture that we will address in part three.

First, I would like to clarify the way I will be using some terms. "Volunteerism" is the act of doing volunteer work in a community. "Voluntourism," a growing trend, is a combination of tourism and volunteer work where an individual or small group decides to do volunteer work during or as a vacation. Finally, the "savior complex" is a belief that an individual is saving or serving others through charity, knowledge, or finances.[29] These are not universal definitions and none of these three concepts has a singular meaning. However, for the purpose of our reflection and discussion, this is how I will be using them in what follows.

Part three is a transition from the first two parts, which focused on prevalent types of considerations before entering into immersive service work. We now shift to

---

29. Some literature refers to this perspective as the "white savior complex" where usually "well-intentioned" white people try to "fix" issues in communities of color. I am using the term "savior complex" instead because I do not want to pigeonhole the phenomenon as an issue that exclusively exists between different racial groups, because it can also be a cultural phenomenon.

looking at the work itself. This material will challenge you to ask hard questions about service and personal motivations. Proceed gently through the material and subsequent conversations that may arise in your immersion groups and service communities. Chapter seven will begin with four case studies on these issues and will examine some of the pros and cons of service work. We will then turn to Scripture in chapter eight and will conclude part three by reflecting on the nuances and tensions of the savior complex in chapter nine. As part three shifts from an inward gaze to an outward one, we now wrestle with the second question offered in the preface: What does it mean to go to the place of another, to immerse yourself in that reality?

Chapter 7

Immersion Case Studies

We begin this chapter with four case studies to guide this part. Unlike the other stories in this book, these scenarios are fictional—although they are similar to things I have witnessed or experienced during immersion work. I invite you to reflect on these examples with your immersion group either prior to traveling to a location or early in the immersive experience. They are not meant to be accusatory. They are meant to help you to explore these issues more deeply. As you read each example, ask yourself if there are components of the story that you find problematic. I will offer my own reflections on the issues presented throughout part three, so I invite you to formulate your own views prior to reading ahead.

Case 1: Hi! My name is Cassie. I am a senior at Pedro Arrupe High School. I love going on service trips and have traveled to Honduras twice. My school has a longstanding relationship with a community in Honduras. While we are there we engage in manual labor, often painting buildings or doing basic landscaping. In the afternoons we spend time with children. This is where I met my friend Isabella. She is *so* wonderful! Both times I saw her I gave her a small gift. It isn't anything expensive, just a small keepsake so she knows I miss her. Isabella is so happy and kind. I can't imagine how she is able to be so happy when there is poverty all around her. She inspires me to be a better person every day, which is why she is in my profile picture on Instagram. I heard about postgraduate volunteer programs from one of my sister's friends. Maybe I'll be able to do one of those in Honduras so I can be closer to Isabella!

Case 2: Hello, my name is Sean. I recently completed my undergraduate study and decided to do a year of postgraduate service in the United States. My placement is at a refugee center. During the day I help process new immigrants and assist them in their search for a home in the city. I also want to be involved in helping residents of this country who are hungry. Twice a week I deliver food to people living on the streets. I usually take the food to places where I know people live and drop it off, even if they aren't there at the time. I wish I could spend time talking to these people, but given my hours at the refugee center I have little time outside of work. At least I know they will have a bit more food to eat.

Case 3: Hello, I'm Colby. I recently completed college and decided to do two years of international service. I felt that it was important to immerse myself in the culture completely. Since arriving in-country a few months ago I adopted the local style of dress and dedicated time to learning the language of the people, and I have a number of local friends who live near the community house. I was recently asked to be a godfather for a newborn baby in the community and I enthusiastically accepted the honor. My perspective is that growing in solidarity with the people means doing everything I can to be like them and to be accepted as one of them. I feel called by God to do this, just as Jesus felt called to spend time with the poor.

Case 4: Hello. My name is Beth. I am a thirty-year-old woman who has made good money through the business world and investments. I am single and want to travel before settling down and starting my family. Although many of my friends encouraged me to take a cruise and travel the world, I decided to spend a few months doing service. I plan to visit one community in Africa and one in South America. At these communities I will volunteer my time and money toward helping children. I am even open to the possibility of adopting a child from one of these countries. Adoption is a beautiful thing and I want to give a child the same opportunities that I had growing up. I don't want to create expectations but want to simply go and help people. This is a far better use of my money than a cruise!

All four of these cases have positive aspects. On the surface, the protagonists wish to help others. However, there are also aspects that could be morally problematic. Take time to consider the strengths and points of growth that are represented in each one before reading on. The next two sections will give macro-level arguments for and against service work before the subsequent chapters unpack some of the specific issues in the case studies.

To Hell with Good Intentions

One of the most articulate expressions of the potential pitfalls of collegiate immersion programs came from Craig, one of my students at John Carroll University. Craig and I often discussed immersion programs and the way they were structured. He disagreed with the fundamental principles of these programs because he felt they always focused on the students who were preparing for the experience. "We treat people like they are in a zoo," he once told me. We take students to a given place, show off the native people and their problems, feel bad for a few days, and then return home. He acknowledged that sometimes students are transformed by the experience, which can have a good long-term effect for them. But a discussion based on outcomes for participants leads back to the same issue. He felt immersions use people to increase the education and diversification of others. It is important to mention that Craig volunteered for two months in Haiti to help people recover after the devastating earthquake in 2010. So, it was not that he was against service in general, but against programs that were designed around the person going into the country, rather than focused on doing service to help others.

Craig was certainly not the first person to warn about the potential dangers of immersions. In 1968 Monsignor Ivan Illich spoke at the Conference on InterAmerican Student Projects in Cuernavaca, Mexico. Knowing he was speaking to young people who were preparing to spend their summer volunteering, Illich implored them to give up on their idea of service in Mexico. His address, although dated in some areas, is an important voice in anti-volunteerism literature. Every volunteer should read Illich before going into a time of service. Although I disagree with parts of his argument and would challenge others, overall, his perspective spurs key questions that are central to grappling with the morality of immersion work.

Illich's address, entitled "To Hell with Good Intentions," makes numerous claims about how service work is harmful. First, he claims it is detrimental to those who are participating in the immersion experience, especially people from the United States who go to another country. These volunteers think they are spreading American ideals to the "less fortunate." He explains, "And it is profoundly damaging to yourselves when you define something that you want to do as 'good,' a 'sacrifice' and 'help.'"[30] When people imagine themselves doing something good for someone else, it builds them up so they can look in the mirror and congratulate themselves for a job well done. This delusion is harmful for a person's development and self-image because they picture themselves as better than others and as the one bringing "help" from a position of superiority.

Second, and more importantly, it is harmful to those the service-provider is there to "save." He states, "All you will do in a Mexican village is create disorder."[31] Volunteers

---

30. Ivan Illich, "To Hell with Good Intentions," delivered April 20, 1968, in Cuernavaca, Mexico, www.uvm.edu/~jashman/CDAE195_ESCI375/To%20Hell%20with%20Good%20Intentions.pdf.

31. Illich, "To Hell with Good Intentions," 3.

come into an area bringing American values and offering to "save" or do good works, but then soon return to their middle-class neighborhoods. Illich says that after these people go home, they continue to make disparaging jokes about Mexicans and those they worked with during their "vacation." He goes on to say that those volunteering rarely learn the language or customs of the people and can only communicate with middle- or upper-class Mexicans. However, they claim their desire is to be present to the "poor," who have no say in allowing them to be there. He emphatically asserts, "It is incredibly unfair for you to impose yourselves on a village where you are so linguistically deaf and dumb that you don't even understand what you are doing, or what people think of you."[32] Finally, Illich says it makes no difference if you live in huts for a week trying to be more like the people around you. Aside from being picturesque, it helps no one.

Illich encourages his audience to visit Mexico, to learn about its history and culture, and to spend tourist dollars there on vacations. What he does not want is "do-gooders" coming to save Mexicans from their poverty because of a sense of self-righteousness. Doing something nice for the "poor" and sacrificing one's summer means nothing and does more harm than good. Sure, the intentions of his audience are likely good, and wanting to help people is important, but the money spent on sending people into other countries could be much better spent on either alleviating the poverty

---

32. Illich, "To Hell with Good Intentions," 5.

of one's own country or developing systems in the United States to solve problems on a grander scale.

Voluntourism, which was described in the fourth case study, suffers from many of the issues that both Illich and Craig described. A common claim against voluntourism is that it exacerbates the disconnection of the "volunteer" from the people. At least on school-sponsored trips, students are often taught about the realities of the place they are going and make some attempt to learn the language and customs. Also, schools often work with existing community partners in the country, so the needs of the location are potentially being met, instead of a well-meaning person building something that is not needed. A wealthy person who shows up in another country looking to spend money and time building something and then leaves soon after can certainly do more harm than good.

The desire to have a few Facebook or Instagram photos of oneself playing with (often) dark-skinned kids whom one perceives as "the poor" exploits those children. In the opening story to part three I described a photograph that was being taken in a train station. What I did not mention is that the background for those photos was Auschwitz. I traveled there with a group of students to learn more about the Holocaust, and as we entered Auschwitz a woman and a photographer were creating a photo shoot. There, in the place where over one million Jews had been killed, were people taking photographs that focused not on the atrocity, but on themselves.

Similar to the photo at Auschwitz, having a picture with a child whom you "love" because you just met them does not mean you want to honor the child. It means you want people to see you working with a child. Holding an umbrella in front of Auschwitz doesn't call to mind the victims of the Holocaust. It shows how nice you look holding an umbrella. I am not claiming that injustice in immersions is the same as the Holocaust. The same would be true for a group of smiling friends giving the thumbs up at the 9/11 Memorial in New York City. I believe taking pictures at Auschwitz or the 9/11 Memorial is okay if the picture does not say "look at me," but rather, "remember what happened here." My point is that some pictures diminish the people, the place, or other subject matter that should be honored in a more dignified way.

Circling back to Illich's original problem, if the immersion or service work isn't about the people, it points back to yourself. Illich and others who concur with his position ask how odd it would be to drive to a poor area of this country, get out of a van, and proceed to play with someone else's children—then take pictures of yourself with them, post them on social media, and leave a short time later. It sounds absurd in the United States, so why does it make a difference if the child is dark-skinned, from a different socio-economic class, of a different religion, or hungry?

Inculturation and Insertion

The Society of Jesus holds a contrary view to Illich on immersion work, which does not mean Jesuits disagree with all of the critiques that Illich offers. However, immersion work has become an important cornerstone for Jesuit high schools and universities, as well as other Catholic and faith-based institutions. To unpack some of the reasons that these experiences are valued, we can turn to two selections by Father Arrupe, addressed to members of the Society of Jesus, and the address by Fr. Peter-Hans Kolvenbach, SJ, at Santa Clara University in 2000. In the documents by Arrupe, he is discussing the importance of inculturation (entering another culture) and insertion experiences (immersion into a particular context) in training Jesuits for missionary work.[33] While the context we are discussing here is more universal in regard to all people who desire to do service work, not necessarily in the context of spreading the Gospel, the insights still hold for our purposes. These three documents bring up important aspects that can address some of Illich's critiques.

The first selection from Arrupe is a letter to the Society of Jesus written in 1978. Arrupe states, "The concepts 'missions,' 'Third World,' 'East/West,' etc. are relative and we should get beyond them, considering the whole world as one single family, whose members are beset by the same varied problems."[34] The realization that these distinctions

---

33. The term "insertion experiences" is outdated and seems to indicate a person is inserted into a community without the permission of the host. This was not Arrupe's intention. "Immersion experiences" is more commonly used today.

34. Pedro Arrupe, S.J., "On Inculturation," in *Other Apostolates Today,* ed. Jerome Aixala, S.J. (St. Louis, MO: The Institute of Jesuit Sources, 1981), 174.

are relative tears down the boundaries that keep us from seeing all people as people of God. Arrupe explains that Christ's presence in all cultures, not just traditionally Western ones, calls us to greater communion with all people. Ignatian spirituality should help in these efforts through multiple ways, such as the universal language of the *Spiritual Exercises*, the Constitutions of the Society of Jesus, and the principles of adaptation found readily in the work of early Jesuit missionaries.[35]

As far as engaging in inculturation, Arrupe writes about the attitudes to have when approaching another culture. Principles of discernment, authenticity, humility, patience, and prudence are all required in this work. Arrupe describes internal consequences for the individual who approaches another culture this way. He says theory and study are not enough to create a change in the individual: "We need the 'shock' of a deep personal experience. For those called to live in another culture, it will mean being integrated into another country, a new language, a whole new life. For those who remain in their own country, it will mean experiencing the new styles of our changing contemporary world."[36] It is not enough to read about something; one must experience it. Arrupe points out that it is not about *being in* another country, but *experiencing* a new culture, regardless of the country. This insertion into another culture "should free us from so much that keeps us

---

35. Arrupe, "On Inculturation," 174–175.
36. Arrupe, "On Inculturation," 179.

shackled."[37] While a delicate task, inculturation can help us see the presence of God in all people across boundaries of culture or country.

The second document is an interview with Arrupe in July 1979. Here, he discusses why exposure to poverty and insertion into poor communities should be experienced by as many Jesuits as possible. Arrupe believes that numerous Jesuits are cut off from experiencing the harshness of life for many people in the world. However, exposure to those experiencing poverty, especially if one has never had this experience, moves them toward an understanding of injustice in a new way. Arrupe explains, "[Insertion experiences] enable us, at least for a time, to get away from a world in which we feel secure, perhaps even comfortable, and experience in our own flesh something of the insecurity, oppression, and misery that is the lot of so many people today. Without such an experience, we cannot really claim to know what poverty is. Still less could we seriously maintain we had made a preferential option for the poor."[38]

In many ways, this statement is the focal point of this book. Immersion work is not only formative for the way one sees the world, but it is also transformative in the way one lives out the Gospel. Arrupe also states that it is not enough to just live in an impoverished place; one must try to share the life of the people and learn from them and their

---

37. Arrupe, "On Inculturation," 179.
38. Pedro Arrupe, S.J., "Exposure To and Insertion Among the Poor," in *Justice with Faith Today*, ed. Jerome Aixala, S.J. (St. Louis, MO: The Institute of Jesuit Sources, 1980), 309.

culture. Without encountering people who have been economically oppressed, a Jesuit is not formed to see the world as Christ did. It is not about being in a physical place, but rather a way of seeing. Using the language of Barron from part one, it is about a movement from the *pusilla anima* to the *magna anima*. It is about metanoia.

Arrupe concludes the interview by offering advice on how to conduct an insertion experience. His tips include: preparation of one's mindset, learning languages and customs, prayer, change in living/working conditions, willingness to serve or be subordinate to those in the community, physical hardship, real poverty, and continued prayer and reflection throughout the experience.[39] The results are often realities people cannot put into words or describe to others. It gives people a deeper sensitivity to others, a keener awareness of the sufferings of those living in poverty and of their own riches, a new awareness of self, and a deeper commitment to others.[40]

From these documents it is clear Arrupe concurs with some of Illich's critiques. For example, both agree that knowledge of a culture and language is important. Illich is upset by people who think they are coming to do "good" for others, while Arrupe stresses it is not about "doing things," but about learning. Humility is important when one enters another culture. Arrupe also emphasizes taking on the real poverty of others, rather than simply living in a hut and eating the same meals as they do. Finally, Arrupe focuses on

---

39. Arrupe, "Among the Poor," 309.
40. Arrupe, "Among the Poor," 312–313.

the long-term transformational aspects of the experience, rather than the short-term goals. While the experiences are still centered on the participant in this framework, Arrupe's words do address *some* of the critiques of immersion work.

The third document is Father Kolvenbach's address at Santa Clara University. As Arrupe's successor as superior general, Kolvenbach sought to strengthen and promote many of Arrupe's views on social justice and solidarity. The third section of his address focuses on the development of Jesuit-educated students and the importance of solidarity in Jesuit education. Kolvenbach places a strong emphasis on an experience of the whole person. He states, "Tomorrow's whole person must have, in brief, a well-educated solidarity."[41] Students should have a greater understanding of the world, other cultures, and how they can contribute to the global community. Learning this solidarity should occur through contact, rather than concepts.[42] This personal contact will challenge students to see "the gritty reality of the world" and to be more knowledgeable about how to respond to this suffering in a personal, individual way. Kolvenbach asserts, "When the heart is touched by direct experience, the mind may be challenged to change. Personal involvement with innocent suffering, with the injustices others suffer, is the catalyst for solidarity, which then gives rise to intellectual inquiry and

---

41. Peter-Hans Kolvenbach, S.J., "The Service of Faith and the Promotion of Justice in American Jesuit Higher Education," in *A Jesuit Education Reader*, ed. George Traub, S.J. (Chicago: Loyola Press, 2008), 155.
42. Kolvenbach, "Service of Faith," 155.

moral reflection."[43] It is not enough to simply learn about injustice, one must encounter it. Through this encounter an individual will be transformed. That is the heart of the Ignatian balance between "the service of faith and the promotion of justice," or, contemplation (the service of faith) in action (justice).

Kolvenbach asserts that the heart of Jesuit education is contact with others that teaches the solidarity of the Gospel. Seeing the world as most people experience it is foundational to understanding that reality beyond what a textbook can show. One can hear stories about suffering, read books on injustice, and hear guest speakers who talk about their lives. These are all movements toward solidarity, a concept that will be explored in part five. But if one wants to come closer to understanding the other, encountering people in the "gritty reality" of their lives will continue to inform one's perspective. The length of time will also play a role. An immersion of ten days will be less transformative than a year or more of service. The longer the experience, the more likely it will be to create an environment where people develop intellectually and morally. Kolvenbach's address and insights on solidarity have greatly influenced the trend toward increasing immersion programs at Jesuit schools.

The transformation of the individual is important for Kolvenbach, as it was for Arrupe. However, does this mean that teachers, campus ministers, and well-meaning people in education are using people who are impoverished? Is

---

43. Kolvenbach, "Service of Faith," 155.

boasting about these programs merely performative, an institutional version of the "look at me" photos described earlier? Do postgraduate volunteer programs use individuals and those in their host countries to generate income to keep their organizations operating? As my student Craig stated, do these trips—or year-long service opportunities—treat people like they are in a zoo to be exploited or commodified for the betterment of wealthier students? These are important considerations. The next two chapters will address these questions through the fictional case studies presented at the start of this chapter.

Reflection Questions

1. Return to the four case studies. Is there one that closely resembles your experience? How can you alter details of the cases to make them better align with the way *you* understand the goal of immersive service work?

2. In what ways have you observed the elements critiqued by Ivan Illich in your program, school, or organization? What concrete solutions can you offer to address Illich's concerns around service experiences and move toward a more holistic Ignatian vision of service?

Chapter 8

An Encounter, Not a Performance

To amalgamate the perspective of Illich with those of Arrupe and Kolvenbach, we begin with prayer. As Arrupe states, any immersion into another culture or way of life should be rooted in prayer. As we examined in the first two parts of the book, prayer invites God into our human experience. In case studies 1, 2, and 4, there is no mention of feeling called by God. Now, "feeling" called by God is not a guarantee of good work, as there are many people who have done horrible things in the name of God. Rather, I suggest that prayer should be the starting point for any volunteer from a faith tradition who is entering a service experience. This is a serious commitment that could negatively impact host communities. The decision should not be taken lightly.

In a short essay, Fr. Frank Wallace, SJ, explains a way to delve deeper into the experience of prayer and how to grow closer to God through prayer. This selection has been very helpful when I present at volunteer orientations. His essay, entitled "Prayer as Encounter and Not Performance," explains the difference between performing and encountering. For example, in a performance, "I" occupy center stage, rather than God. In performance, we wear masks that hide our true selves and there is very little listening. In performance prayer, I do not bring God into the picture but focus only on my needs and wants. Encounter is different. Wallace explains, "There is honest revelation. . . . No pretending to be other than I am. This is authentic . . . and I relate to God as God as well as I can and I allow God to be God. . . . [I]n a true encounter with God or anybody else, the condition is one of freedom and trust."[44] Encounter is about being and loving, allowing God to be God, rather than performing in the hopes of a better reward. Prayer of encounter is the type of prayer needed when entering a service experience or deciding how to live as a volunteer.

Encounter is not only about your relationship with God, but with the people in your community as well. Establishing a relationship of encounter is crucial to an authentic relationship in service. Case study 2 describes Sean working with refugees during the day, which is an important service. In the evenings, wanting to do more, he drops off food to people in need. Again, this is important, but spending time talking to those people, building relationships of encounter, is equally, if not more, important. Charity is good, but charity without relationship can create dependence. In this fictional example, Sean does not have time to talk to people. To rectify this, perhaps he could ask others in his community if they could rotate shifts with him and he could use that opportunity to spend meaning-

---

44. Frank Wallace, S.J., "Prayer as Encounter and Not Performance," in *Encounter Not Performance* (Australia: E.J. Dwyer, 1991), 6.

ful time with people once a week. One of the failings of voluntourism is that people come and go quickly and may not prioritize the depth of relationship between the volunteer and the "one in need." Living a service experience of encounter also includes living simply and trying to live in a process of solidarity in the best way possible.

When Father Gray introduced me to Wallace's essay in a class on Ignatian spirituality, he offered another image to explain the difference between performance and encounter. He asked us to reflect on pilgrims and tourists. The pilgrim, he explained, is one who seeks encounter. She does not know all the answers, but is open to seeing where the journey will go. The pilgrim does not want the comforts of air-conditioning or food similar to that of her country of origin. The tourist, on the other hand, follows strict schedules, wants to take pictures to show people his experiences, hopes for amenities, and does not necessarily want to be changed by the experience. To be a tourist, Gray said, "is like taking a shower with a raincoat on. You want the experience of the shower, but you do not want to get wet." The class giggled at this image, but it has always stuck with me.

While these generalizations are not true for every person, I think he makes a good point. This is not to knock tourism—I have been both a tourist and a pilgrim. Many places around the world are dependent upon tourist dollars to support businesses. As I tell my classes when I teach this lesson, it is not about one practice being bad or good; it is about knowing which you are doing in a given situation and understanding your role. A problem can arise when you are a tourist but you think you are a pilgrim. You return home with pictures of a location and talk to people about your trip as though you know what life is like in that area because you experienced it through a tour bus. This is true of any place, not just countries where people go to "do service."

Case study 4 is about Beth and her desire to engage in voluntourism. I think it is appropriate to address that desire in light of Father Gray's observations. It is certainly possible to be a voluntourist who approaches the experience as an encounter. I do not want to disparage people when I do not know their heart. However, if a person wants to engage in the activities of case study 4, I would hope that sincere reflection accompanies that decision. It, too, is a serious decision to enter into the community of another. This case study represents the greatest potential of falling into Illich's negative characterization of service work. As Arrupe indicates, learning languages and customs is important and should accompany all types of volunteering in whatever way possible.

To illustrate why it is important to know whether you are a tourist or a pilgrim, I would like to offer an example not related to service experiences. I have a friend named Michael who lives in Honolulu. When I visit we usually go into Waikiki for a day or evening, but most of our time is spent driving around the island and meeting people. I have often noticed that many people who go to Honolulu for a vacation rarely leave Waikiki. The beachfront of the beautiful hotels is designed so tourists never have to leave the area. They do not see the "true" aspects of Hawaii and meet very few native Hawaiians, except those who are paid to give them a tour to specific places. Hawaii is a complex place with poverty, injustice, and inequality. Tourists rarely see, for example, the poor communities on the island or the way native Hawaiians are treated. Hawaii is held up as a paradise where everyone lives extravagantly, yet the reality is that many people have to work two or three jobs to afford to live there.

Again, there is nothing wrong with tourism and I am glad so many people go to Hawaii so Michael, who works in the restaurant business, has a job. Sometimes my friends or relatives tell me they experienced Hawaii and assert it is a place without poverty where everyone is happy. But when they proceed to tell me they never left Waikiki, it demonstrates for me the difference between performance and encounter, between the tourist and the pilgrim. The dichotomy between performance and encounter is, I believe, central to the debate about volunteerism and voluntourism. Determining if you are a pilgrim or a tourist in the way you approach service is important. Are you trying to see the truth of the people, culture, and way of life that is offered to you as a gift?

The Poor Widow's Contribution

"The people are so poor, but they are so happy! They give us so much, even though they have so little!" In case study 1, Cassie comments on how her friend Isabella is so welcoming. I often hear this assertion when I lead immersions.

However, this reaction to immersion work has become like fingernails on a chalkboard for many people in social justice circles. I suspect that many of you have either said this or know people who have said it. An immersion participant is only with a person for a few hours at a time over a brief period. It is a short snapshot of a person's experience. Visiting a friend once a week for a few hours and seeing how happy they are to have company does not mean you know that that person lives a happy life. It could be that your friend, or someone you visit on an immersion, is only truly happy when you are present. We should not make assumptions about people's lives, especially when we do not know them personally.

I do not dispute that people who are materially poor can be happy and can give freely, and can do so with joy. I do dispute that these are all connected in the way the speaker often means—that *because* these people have so little, their lives are so much better. I hear students then reflect, "Perhaps I do not need all the things in my life." This is a great realization! Being inspired to live more simply is a great lesson to take away from an immersion. I think the best way to honor someone who is materially poor and joyful is to say, "Despite experiencing poverty and injustice, these people teach us that moments of joy are still possible"—the point being, they are not happy because they are poor or marginalized. They are happy *despite* their experience of injustice and/or poverty.

In the Gospel of Mark chapter 12, there is a short narrative about Jesus observing a poor widow donating money in the Temple. While the rich put in a lot of money, the poor widow put in two coins, her whole livelihood. Jesus points this out to the disciples. He says that this woman has given everything. In homilies the preacher often muses that Jesus is praising the woman and that her faith is so great that she trusts God will take care of her. Giving everything you have is held up to be a great standard. If giving everything one has is the most godly action, it would seem that everyone, including those experiencing poverty, should be encouraged to give up what little they have to please God. However, that is ridiculous. I do not know of anyone who would say the best place to raise money for a cause, even a religious one, is among people who have no money.

Father Gray once preached on this Gospel passage and offered a nuanced interpretation that differed from the usual perspective. He said that we cannot tell what Jesus' tone is when he calls the disciples to observe the widow. We assume Jesus is happy and congratulatory toward what he witnesses, but he could also be angry. If you reread the story and imagine Jesus speaking in a harsh and angry tone, it still fits with the words. Gray concluded that Jesus is actually disheartened with the scene, as the woman has been conditioned into thinking she should give all that she has to the religious institution. Who will support her when she needs to eat that night? We should never expect those experiencing poverty to give everything they have, and neither would Jesus, Gray explained to us.

Being impoverished doesn't make one happy. Neither the widow nor the people one encounters on an immersion trip are happy because they are poor. Living simply certainly can make one happy. Less reliance on technology, status, and wealth are good lessons. However, not having enough money to feed your family, not having safety or shelter, being abused or forgotten—these conditions should not be idolized in a fanciful way. Jesus was not happy watching a "poor widow" give up her last coins. We need to work to correct the presumptions that poverty results in people being kinder and more joyful.

Reflection Questions

1. In what areas outside of service have you experienced the dichotomy between "encounter versus performance" and "tourist versus pilgrim"?

2. Have you ever believed, or heard someone else express, that "the poor are so happy, because they have nothing"? Is there a better way to express this idea that fits with the context you experienced in service?

Chapter 9

Intentionality and the Moral Choice

Intentionality is an important aspect of Catholic ethics in general, and it is also an important question to revisit daily when doing immersion and service work. Each person in the case studies seems to have different intentions, but there is not enough information to know how the volunteer arrived at these decisions. Beth, in case study 4, has money and wants to spend it on others. Colby and Sean want to experience long-term service and Cassie wants to support her young friend who lives in another country. All can be good motivations for service work, but all can also be harmful motivations. Prayer, as mentioned previously, is important for discerning your motivations for doing service. Do you intend to engage in this work for the reasons that Illich describes—essentially, to make yourself feel better? Or are you doing it so others will think more highly of you? These can be problematic intentions for doing service work.

My former student, Craig, believed immersion work as it is presented in many high schools and colleges is very "me" focused. In some ways, I agree with him. Couching the experience as "giving to others," whether the gift is your time or money, creates a secondary intention in order to ease the primary one—*I* want to see the other, visit another culture, meet new people, etc. I do not think this makes all immersion work harmful, but it's an important question to ask yourself before, during, and after an experience: Why did I do this? Hopefully people of faith root their desire in the texts and teachings of their religious tradition. For many Christians, this is expressed as a desire to follow the example of Jesus. I do not think that description has one answer, but I think it is a starting point. The specifics of how you act, whether as a self-inflated "savior" or humble learner, can make or break the experience as an encounter of authenticity.

The intention of the trip itself can be just as important as the intention of the volunteer. For example, Craig wanted to go to Haiti to clean up after the earthquake to help other people recovering from a disaster. A retired staff member at John Carroll, Tom Reilley, traveled to New Orleans for many years helping to clean up after the flooding from Hurricane Katrina. Although he did spend time creating "encounter, not performance" relationships with the people he helped, it was not central to his immersion trip. Usually, when one goes into another culture to live or work, the focus is on the person. However, when one mobilizes people to clean up after a disaster, the disaster is the focus. I make this distinction because I do not think Illich had these sorts of trips in mind when giving his critique. A group who goes to New Orleans or Haiti may be "do-gooders," but the good they are doing is measurable: helping people get back to a status they had, rather than a desired status perpetrated by a savior mentality. Of course, cleanup should be coordinated with or by people of that community, but my point is that volunteers are there primarily to do a concrete task that returns people to what they lost in life, not to build a new *way* of life.

These trips could be considered forms of charity, while most immersions are aimed at social justice. This distinction is also important. Charity is not a bad thing, especially in the wake of a natural disaster. Works of charity are part of the Christian tradition. However, charity without justice can create situations of dependence that do not get to the root of the problem. Working for justice, which is also part of the Christian tradition, requires asking why the need for charity exists. Hopefully, immersion programs or postgraduate volunteer organizations challenge participants to move to this level of education and examination.

A second example of intention involves focusing on educating participants so they can join in advocacy efforts and educate others when they return home. An example is traveling to Immokalee, Florida, to learn about the unjust immigration system in the United States. While volunteers are visiting the Coalition of Immokalee Workers, a group that acts as a union for documented and undocumented farmworkers, we are told to take pictures, ask questions, post things to social media, and get the word out about what is happening. Although I generally think being away from technology and being careful about picture-taking is important during an immersion, there are also circumstances where these actions are encouraged. And as always, this should be approached carefully and on a case-by-case basis.

Intention does not always make something right, in both Catholic ethics and service work. In case study 3, Colby has a desire to grow closer to his community, which is a great intention. However, some may have read that case and felt he went too far. Intention alone does not make an action moral, just as it does not always make a decision during service appropriate. Again, this isn't to say that all of Colby's actions are wrong. However, one should proceed with caution so as not to move too fast to become part of a culture. While you may not have years to spend waiting, you should not rush to ingratiate yourself. This should always be done in response to an invitation to grow closer to another and, when the invitation is given, one should proceed with care and prudence. Some programs would not allow a volunteer to become a godparent to a local child, for example, because the volunteer is eventually going to return to their home country. Once that happens, the well-intentioned volunteer may never see the child again, and having a godparent who can only serve in a purely honorific role (instead of regular personal involvement) could cause sadness from the child or resentment from the parents. The intention is thoughtful, but the action may have unforeseen consequences on that community and family.

Cultural Tension of Being a Savior

While some situations are more clearly examples of the savior complex, others are ambiguous. There are times when the savior complex manifests itself not as a desire to improve structures or to hold babies, but to correct behavior that a volunteer feels goes against their own moral fiber. There are many examples of how this can occur, but I will share two that have been very difficult for me to reconcile. I hope that you are able to put any similar issues that you face or have faced into conversation with these examples. In many cases, it is a balance between your role as a volunteer and your sense of morality. I do not think there are easy answers to these questions and I hope these examples lead to discussions within your communities about why you think certain actions should or should not be taken.

In 2013 I traveled to Ecuador a second time to lead a retreat for *Rostro de Cristo* volunteers. During a session about suffering, one of the volunteers, Ana, shared with us that one of her difficulties was knowing how to act in the face of domestic abuse. When a woman comes to the shelter where Ana is working and relays to her how her husband beats her when he is drinking, what should she, as a volunteer, do? Her heart tells her that she should encourage the woman to leave her husband and to take her children away. Her American education has encouraged a mindset that empowers women and she has encountered many resources in her life in America that make her believe that help is possible. However, in Ecuador, the culture is quite different. Often these women have no way to support themselves and if they leave their husbands there are few places they can go. The strong machismo culture of the region prioritizes masculine values (the kind that Americans might consider stereotypical or even "toxic"), and women are unlikely to be willing to leave these men, even if they are being abused. This issue has come up in every retreat I have led in Ecuador since. But this was the first time I had been asked this question, and I was silent.

Before unpacking this issue, I want to clarify that this question has many layers. First, Ecuador is not a country where "every man" abuses women. Violence against women is not a Latin American problem; it is a human problem. The difference between Ecuador and, say, the United States, is that there are more resources available to women in the United States who are victims of abuse. Second, when I say that this is an issue of deciding the right course of action, I do not mean that we should condone violence against women, or anyone. The question is not if abuse is warranted. The question is, what should Ana, or any volunteer living in another country, do when they encounter abuse. Ultimately, the question is, what is the role of a volunteer?

Before going further with Ana's question, I want to offer the second example. When I traveled to Tanzania in 2017 to co-facilitate a retreat for the Jesuit Volunteers there, I learned a lot about the country and some of the injustices faced by its people. My co-facilitator Michele Shimizu-Kelley and I created a space for the volunteers to explain some of their difficult experiences. One of the prominent difficulties was the prevalence of corporal punishment at the schools where the volunteers taught. While the volunteers were not expected to hit the children with the stick, they were often present for these beatings. Given that many, if not all, of the volunteers that year were raised in households that forbade corporal punishment, this was difficult for them to process.

One of the volunteers who struggled the most with this practice was Garrett. Garrett's story was both insightful and powerful. As a teacher, he would use his iPod to play music during class. One day, he discovered the iPod was missing; he was pretty sure which student had taken it based on who was in the vicinity when it disappeared. When he questioned the student, the student denied taking it. Later, a fellow volunteer found the iPod in the student's possession and returned it to Garrett, leaving it to his discretion on how the situation should be handled. Garrett then called the student into his office to sort out what had happened. Although the student continuously denied it, Garrett knew he had done it. Garrett understood that the young man was adamantly denying it in fear of being punished (i.e., beaten). To find a middle ground, Garrett told the student that the incident would need to be reported to administration in order to keep records on student behavior, but if he admitted his guilt Garrett would ask the administration not to cane him. In tears, the student finally confessed and Garrett thanked him for his honesty.

Garrett knew the proper protocol was to report the theft to the dean of students, but he suspected it would lead to the child being beaten. After grappling with the appropriate action, he hesitantly reported the incident. However, he asked that the child not be punished and assured the dean that their conversation over the matter would suffice and he saw that the student was truly remorseful. His superior agreed and called in the young man. During this discussion, the student once again admitted to taking the iPod. Following this admission, the dean beat the student with the stick, despite his assurance to Garrett that the child would not be physically punished. After the incident, the student returned to Garrett's office hysterical and feeling incredibly betrayed due to Garrett's assurance that he would not be beaten. In bringing this story to our group, Garrett had many questions he was working through. Because he reported the theft, was he complicit in the physical abuse? Should he be upset that he was lied to by the superior? The scenario and his guilt were complex issues pointing to a deeper question about his role as a volunteer in Tanzania.

These two stories have similarities and differences. One difference is that some readers may support corporal punishment and therefore have less aversion toward the Tanzanian school's policy. I am hopeful that no readers sanction spousal abuse. Another difference is that Garrett witnessed the beatings, while Ana only heard stories. It is possible that witnessing something can cause you to go numb to it over time. Although this was not the case with Garrett, it could certainly be that way with other volunteers who daily witness things that they once found morally repugnant. And finally, Garrett's situation was sanctioned by law and was part of the culture, while Ana's, although cultural, was still not viewed favorably by average Ecuadorians. Parents knew that their child could be punished this way in the school and that it was part of school policy.

Despite these differences, I think the underlying question is the same: Should Ana and/or Garrett intervene in the activity that they found immoral? The social-justice-minded person may initially want to say, "Yes, of course, when someone is being physically abused it is our role, formed in the spirit of the Gospel, to help the victim." But it is not that easy.

First, we have to ask ourselves: What is the role of a volunteer in a country? Volunteers are there to offer presence, but not to police or impress values on another culture. This is the definition of the savior complex. It is easy to say we should not force people to eat the same foods, or build their homes a certain way. It is much harder to step back when it is a moral issue that "we" think is "obvious." Second, we can do more harm than good by imposing "our" values on others. The woman who leaves her husband has nowhere to go. Telling children that they should stand up to adults because they should not be beaten might undo layers of respect built into a culture. Third, those involved in a service experience do not have all the answers. They are outsiders to a culture. That does not mean context can excuse physical violence. Rather, it means that the volunteers can't control the long-term outcome of their actions because they will eventually return home. Their time in the location is finite, especially for a short-term immersion. And fourth, a volunteer's actions will have an impact on the program and subsequent volunteers. A volunteer is part of a chain uniting the past and the future, and every action can disturb the balance of a society and have ramifications long after a volunteer returns home.

With that said, I do not think a volunteer is powerless. There is a model of suffering presence that will be discussed in part four. I think creativity is important too. Ana and other volunteers have encouraged and supported the formation of support groups for women so they know they are not alone. These support groups are not dependent on the volunteers, but on the Ecuadorian women themselves. This is crucial. The volunteers may not be able to solve the problem, but they can encourage systems of support that are grounded in existing communities. Ana certainly had the resources and support of her supervisors at her placement and within *Rostro de Cristo*. As for Garrett, he did his best not to be present for the beatings. He also talked to adults about why corporal punishment was part of the culture. When appropriate, he challenged them to think about other options, but he did not openly defy the school in front of the children. He also supported the children with love after the punishments, in the same way Ana showed love to the women who were abused.

The examples from Ana and Garrett are small snapshots from one or two years of service in Ecuador and Tanzania. Having worked with them at multiple points during their service experiences, I can attest to the fact that they valued their time as volunteers and would not want these examples to be the only things you remember about these cultures. Their love for the people is what made these experiences so difficult. I hope that readers who are not familiar with these cultures realize that there is far more to Ana's and Garrett's experiences. I would also like to point out that their organizations do have structures to help deal with these difficult decisions. The volunteers are not left to ask these moral questions alone. Ultimately, however, it is the volunteers who must wrestle with the morality of what they observe and experience, and that is why I offered these difficult and challenging stories. You, no doubt, may have your own moments of moral indecision and I offer this section to affirm that you are not alone in your effort to live within the tension between your moral compass and your volunteer commitment.

Throughout much of this book I endeavor to not create a divide between service inside the United States and service in other countries. However, in this case a distinction is important. While there are situations where one should not force morals upon a community in the United States, there are also legal ramifications for not reporting abuse. So, while I think deciding what can be done in cases of abuse when immersed in another culture is a gray area, it is not a gray area in the United States. Abuse should be reported to your organization, and those who run the program can best decide how to proceed so you are not in danger of retribution. Your safety is important as well.

Reflection Questions

1. Is it possible to have an immersion program that does not treat people like they are "in a zoo" if it is focused on the development of the one engaged in the experience? If so, how do you think it should be coordinated?

2. Do you agree with my conclusions regarding Ana's and Garrett's experiences? If not, what do you think is the best way to approach these difficult questions?

3. If you are on a short-term immersion trip or long-term immersive experience, what are you trying to accomplish? Take time to journal about this question. Would that answer have been different one month ago? Or one year ago? Take time to discuss this answer with those in your community.

Conclusion

People Aren't a Photo Op

This chapter awakens in me realizations about how wrong I have been in my own work with students. During my first trip to Immokalee I valued having a picture of me reading with a young student of color while we were doing after-school tutoring. This is similar to Cassie in the first case study. The picture ended up being used for an advertisement for the trip in a school publication. Although I did not know this was going to happen, at the time, I felt no shame in its publication. There I was, "saving" the world, one dark-skinned child at a time. I spent only twenty minutes with this child listening to him read me a story, but somehow, I felt the picture was appropriate.

On many subsequent trips to Immokalee I made sure to get pictures of my students in action. We always asked permission of the school and if it was a picture of a student standing with a child, we asked the child. Sometimes the children said no. Likely, though, most children do not really comprehend the ramifications of consenting to such a photograph. I then gave my students the pictures, along with many others from the week, as a way to remember their experience. While I had realized by this time that I did not want pictures of myself with kids that I only knew for a short time, I was still clueless as to why taking these pictures for my students could be harmful. I now believe the harm outweighs any good. I was the same as the woman in the opening story of part three, who wanted a picture with the Auschwitz train station in the background while she was the main attraction. For both of us, the focus was on "me," an experience of performance, rather than encounter. In this way, I was exploiting children for my own gain.

Another difficult question around photographs arose when I traveled to Tanzania. When I was at an outdoor bus station awaiting travel back to Dar es Salaam, I took a picture of the bus station. I partly wanted a picture of the sign written in Swahili, but I also was amazed at the way the station operated as buses seamlessly pulled in and out without centralized coordination. One of my friends, Patrice, chastised me for taking the picture. On the ten-hour bus ride we had an honest and vulnerable conversation about why it offended her. Patrice had been living in the country for almost two years and was nearly finished with her JVC international service commitment. Tanzania and the people of the country had truly become part of her identity and she felt that taking this picture was exploiting a difference between the American way of life and the Tanzanian way of life. While I acknowledged that pictures of people would fall into this category, I felt the picture of the bus station would not. We ended the conversation agreeing to disagree. I appreciated that she brought this to light because otherwise I would not have thought about that perspective. As I look back at our discussion now, I am reminded of the importance of trusting those who have been in a country longer or those who live there to explain what is or is not appropriate behavior. While I was not convinced of Patrice's position, it is better to be overly humble and respectful, rather than less so. I think this approach is a good starting point as you figure out what photos are appropriate in your service context.

Part three has explored a number of difficult topics with no easy answers. I hope it is the start of conversations for you and not the conclusion. In navigating the tensions between Illich and Arrupe/Kolvenbach, begin with prayer. Through prayer, you may see people you meet who radiate joy, not as a caricature of their poverty, but as human beings as complex as you, human beings who are made in the image of God. Daily reviewing your intentions and the intentions of your program will hopefully help you live into this realization. Finally, remember the great privilege that allows you to enter into the reality of another so that the photos you take honor the authenticity of the person, rather than commodify their skin color or socio-economic status. We are beginning to answer the question from the preface: What does it mean to go into the place of another? In this space, not charted or mapped out, you could find an encounter that radically changes your perception of the world and the people in it.

Part Four

A Suffering Presence

In 2006 I took a road trip to St. Louis with two friends. Halfway through our excursion I received a phone call from my roommate Dragan. His father, barely fifty years old, had suffered a severe stroke the previous night and wasn't found until morning. The prognosis was bleak. He was unresponsive, in a coma, and doctors believed he would never regain consciousness. My friends and I agreed that we would leave immediately and drive through the night to get back to Cleveland. After driving nine hours we arrived the next morning. For most of the drive I had been silent, pondering what I would say to my friend. How could I help alleviate the suffering wound upon his soul as his father fought for his life? I was not a doctor and had no idea of the likelihood of his recovery. The usual platitudes of "It will be okay" seemed insincere and hollow.

This part of the book will take up the issue of suffering, or, at the very least, will offer a few perspectives on how to process some of the suffering that is encountered during an immersion experience or time of service. The questions I wrestled with as we drove to Cleveland may be similar to the questions on the minds of those who immerse themselves into a place where suffering is great. Often, there is little a volunteer can do in the moment to "fix" an injustice or difficult situation they encounter, just as there was little I could say to my friend to take away the pain of his father's condition. There are times when we are called to act, to fix situations or help others. However, in the context of being in a community or country that is not your own, taking action to "correct" problems or "fix" a situation needs to be handled gingerly, as we discussed in part three. Moving from contemplating your role in another country, we now focus on processing experiences where we feel powerless in the face of suffering. If Ana and Garrett should not step in to stop the abuse they witnessed, what should they do? How can one react in the face of powerlessness? Part four will offer psychological and theological observations, drawing from experience, the Gospel, and our limited understanding of the mystery of God.

Chapter 10

A Binder and a Bag of Rocks

In 2013 I was privileged to meet a man named Paul Fugelsang. Paul is a psychotherapist who specializes in treating anxiety, depression, and trauma. Our paths crossed, however, not in the world of psychology, but each summer as we both presented at the Jesuit Volunteer Corps International and *Rostro de Cristo* orientation. He offered two images during his sessions with the volunteers to prepare them for entry into their host countries and I think his insights will be a particularly helpful way to begin our reflections on suffering.

Paul began his session by explaining his own background as a volunteer who served in Peru for two years with JVC. One of the stories he told involved a woman named Juana, who sold corn-flavored juice called *chicha* to support her family. One day she was unable to pay her electric bill, which meant she could not keep the juice in her refrigerator cool. If the juice was not cool, she would be unable to sell it and make money. She feared what this would mean for her livelihood. Paul explained that he immediately went into problem-solving mode, trying to help this woman come up with alternatives for how to keep her produce fresh. He then stopped the story and invited the volunteers to reflect on what he did and if there was another way he could have approached the situation.

Sometimes, the volunteers understood what Paul was getting at, while other times they were unsure. "She did not need me to come up with snap solutions," he explained. "She simply needed me to sit with her in her pain." In order to illustrate this, Paul would invite a volunteer to come forward and hold a binder above his or her head. He explained that this binder represents the suffering any of us feel in a given moment. Sometimes it is low and easy to carry; other times it feels like a tremendous weight bearing down on us. He would then attempt to pull the binder away, throwing the person off balance. "Is this helping you hold it up?" he would inquire. Clearly, it made the binder harder to hold. He would then stop pulling and place one finger under the binder to help remove a small fraction of the weight. "How about now?" The person would always respond in the affirmative. "This is our hope—if we are lucky, it might help to relieve a small amount of their burden," he concluded.

To further illustrate this lesson, Paul would offer the image of a bag of rocks, and sometimes bring a plastic bag with crumpled paper to appear as rocks. "We all carry around a bag of rocks," he would explain. "Sometimes it is heavy, sometimes it is light. We have the opportunity to remove rocks from or add rocks to other people's bags each day." For example, being supportive of someone may take away a rock. On the contrary, yelling at someone and adding stress to their life would add to the weight of their bag. He concluded by suggesting that we never know the weight of someone's bag and should always be careful in taking actions that could add rocks to the bag of another—and realize that sometimes we do this inadvertently.

These are not just important points for a time of service, but for life. The way we impact others can be detrimental in ways that we do not realize. Even when, with the best intentions, we try to take away someone's suffering, it can make the person's life harder, their bag of rocks heavier. However, the one finger pushing the binder gently upward symbolizes sitting with the person in that pain. It is a small gesture that will not take away the pain, but it will remind the person that they are not sitting in that pain alone.

When I first heard Paul's presentation I thought back to those moments when I walked up the steps at Dragan's parents' house years ago. When I saw Dragan we hugged and walked to his father's bedroom. We sat on the bed in silence. Over the next hour and thirty minutes we spoke perhaps two sentences to each other. And we sat. I kept telling myself I was doing something through my silence, despite the urge to speak, which was nearly overwhelming. Eventually, Dragan stood. I stood. We hugged again and then walked to the kitchen where his mother had made us dinner. For the rest of the evening we did not talk about his father or the tragedy of his stroke. I did my best to take Dragan's mind off his pain through small talk and remained with him for much of the evening.

It was many months before his father surprised the doctors by coming out of his coma. Years later, Dragan and I spoke on the phone. He told me, "I want to thank you for the day you sat with me after my father's stroke.

I knew you didn't know what to say, but you sat there. I knew you cared about us because you sat there." I took a deep breath and had to pause before I could reply. I thanked him and explained that sitting there was the only thing I could think to do. That was the most powerful instance in my life where I learned the importance of being present to the suffering in the life of another while also being powerless to change a situation. This experience taught me to not attempt to rip the binder of pain from another's hands, but to lift a finger in support, because it means far more to the one in pain.

Suffering Presence

Paul's advice to volunteers is an important psychological insight for understanding the harmful effects of trying to take away another person's suffering. There are also theological perspectives that echo Paul's approach. One text that elucidates the power of sitting with someone in their pain is *Suffering Presence*. The author, Stanley Hauerwas, is a well-known Methodist scholar who has written extensively on issues of politics, war and peace, and suffering. I had read this book a few years before Dragan's father's stroke. Of all the "tools" I had acquired at that point in my life to help me decide what to say to Dragan, Hauerwas's insights were the most helpful. We will briefly unpack Hauerwas' sperspectives before applying them to the experience of suffering in immersion work.

In the third chapter of *Suffering Presence*, Hauerwas explicates his concept of being a "suffering presence" for someone—being present with them and to them when they are suffering—through an analysis of the question, "Why does medicine need the church?" In order to explain what he means, he begins with the book of Job, a book in the Old Testament known for the way it attempts to address the problem of evil. The protagonist, Job, loses his land and his loved ones. At first, his friends sit with him, but later they say God must be punishing him, if these things are happening. Hauerwas uses the example of Job's friends to discuss the importance of being present. While pain often serves to isolate people, Job's friends decided to sit with him. Hauerwas explains, "They sat on the ground with Job doing nothing more than being willing to be present in the face of his suffering."[45] Although they later ridicule Job and blame him for his losses, Hauerwas points out that their first action is to sit with their friend.

After reflecting on Job, Hauerwas shares a similar story about himself and his friend Bob. Bob's mother died by suicide and Hauerwas explains how he sat with his friend in his pain. He says, "I felt awkward, but I went. . . . We never talked about his mother or what had happened." He could not help Bob, nor explain why his mother would do such a horrible thing. All he could do was be present.[46] From his

---

45. Stanley Hauerwas, *Suffering Presence: Theological Reflections on Medicine, the Mentally Handicapped, and the Church* (Notre Dame, Indiana: University of Notre Dame Press, 1986), 78.
46. Hauerwas, *Suffering Presence*, 78.

personal example and his observation about Job, Hauerwas makes a case that there is something important about being present, intentionally and attentively focusing on the presence of the other, with those who are suffering. Not because words can take away the pain, but because it is a powerful experience to offer to share that pain. As Paul Fugelsang said, people sometimes need a person to simply sit with them.

Hauerwas then moves to a discussion on the role of the church as a community to embody this reality. Physicians are trained to be present in the face of suffering, but they cannot sustain this presence indefinitely. There is a limit to the capabilities of medicine and eventually conditions deteriorate beyond medicine's ability to provide resolutions. Those who have accompanied others in death or who have worked with hospice patients know the limitations of medicine and the power of presence during these times. Hauerwas contends that, in the face of these struggles, someone or something else is needed to sustain this care. This entity, he believes, is the church. Hauerwas observes, "Thus medicine needs the church not to supply a foundation for its moral commitments, but rather as a resource of the habits and practices necessary to sustain the care of those in pain over the long haul."[47] The church should be a collection of people who do not let pain and suffering become excuses for ostracization, but instead, invitations for companionship.

Prayer, sometimes viewed as a final option for a cure, is also important in Hauerwas's perspective, but for differ-

---

47. Hauerwas, *Suffering Presence*, 81.

ent reasons. He explains, "For prayer is not a supplement to the insufficiency of our medical knowledge and practice; nor is it some divine insurance policy that our medical skill will work; rather, our prayer is the means that we have to make God present whether our medical skill is successful or not."[48] A community for whom prayer is a central component to its existence, such as the church, understands that the importance of prayer isn't based on the outcome, but rather, on the presence of God in the life of the community. Hauerwas explains that the church is a group of people who have learned to embody such a presence in their lives to the point that it has "become the marrow of their habits."[49] In short, the church should be the group that embodies the teachings of the Gospel to be present to the stranger and to sit by the side of those who suffer, no matter how bleak the medical prognosis may seem.

Applying Hauerwas's perspective to a volunteer's experience is possible whether the volunteer program is overtly religious or secular. Although this is easier to conceptualize within, and may be a more welcome analysis for, a Christian service program, nearly all service programs would concur that teaching their volunteers how to be present to suffering is an important component of formation. Especially in Christian programs, volunteers can draw inspiration from Jesus' love for others and can be encouraged to be present in the face of injustices that cannot be reconciled. This is not to say that all immersion participants are overtly Christian

---

48. Hauerwas, *Suffering Presence*, 81.
49. Hauerwas, *Suffering Presence*, 80.

or religious. However, they can be informed by the spirit of the Gospel, called to be present where suffering is greatest.

Reflection Questions

1. Have you had the experience of being a suffering presence to another person? Has anyone ever been a suffering presence for you? Take time to reflect on this experience and the lessons you learned about yourself and being present to others.

2. Immersion groups and volunteer communities require balance, care, and support. What have you found that adds rocks to or removes rocks from the bag of your community or group? In what ways can you be a suffering presence to others in your service group?

Chapter 11

The Consolation of the Gospel

Hauerwas's reliance on the church as a suffering presence for those in need is rooted in the Gospel accounts of Jesus' life. One could point to many relevant passages; I wish to offer two to demonstrate that Jesus was a suffering presence to those he encountered. The first is from one of the many healing narratives found in the Gospels. The second is the appearance of the risen Jesus on the road to Emmaus. Bringing consolation as a suffering presence in the lives of others is clearly articulated in the mission of Christ, both during his earthly life and following his resurrection.

Luke 13 tells the story of Jesus healing a crippled woman on the Sabbath. Jesus was teaching in a synagogue. There was a woman there who had been bent over, crippled by a spirit, unable to stand erect. The text explains that Jesus saw her, called to her, and then laid hands upon her. We should note, first, that the synagogue where Jesus was teaching would have been divided by sex, with men on one side and women on the other. Second, believing this woman to be possessed by an evil spirit meant that Jewish cleanliness laws would have dictated that she be away from others, perhaps in the very back of the worship space. And third, the description of the woman as bent over by a spirit reveals that she would not have been able to look up to see people without pain, if at all. If you have ever seen a person who looks to the ground because of a spinal condition, you have an idea of this woman's condition. She was physically unable to see the community.

These details are all important for understanding Jesus' actions. First, he sees her. The unclean and the marginalized are often ignored in society, both then and now. As you walk down the street take notice of how the average person reacts when they see a person begging on the side of the road. Often they walk by, trying to ignore the person. And so, this woman, deemed unclean by society, would have often been ignored. Yet, Jesus sees her. Second, he calls to her, making a public display and providing confirmation that she is seen. He does not keep this to himself, but lets everyone know that he has seen her. He does not hide or bury his reaction. And third, he lays his hand on her. It would have been unusual for a man to touch a woman who was not his wife in such a public display, and even more so because she is unclean. Jewish law dictated that Jesus would now be unclean too. Yet, he takes on this uncleanliness. He shares the burden.

The next moment is often the focus of the passage. The woman stands straight and glorifies God. One can contend, however, that the miracle was completed before her spine was made straight. In fact, if you do not believe in physical miracles or healings, I challenge you to still see a miraculous event here. A woman who was crippled, discarded by society, pushed to the back of the synagogue, was recognized. She was affirmed. She was seen. Jesus became her suffering presence. I think this is important for us to understand because I know that *I* can't heal spinal conditions with a touch. Belief in Jesus' ability to do so does not change my inability to do it. I can, however, see someone who is pushed aside, call out to them, and take the risk of sharing their burden. We do not need to be the Son of God to accomplish miracles.

The other passage I wish to reflect on is Luke 24. In the well-known account of the road to Emmaus, Jesus approaches his disciples and brings them consolation. At the start of the passage we are told that the two disciples are downcast. Again, by using our imagination and understanding the position of this story in Scripture we can deepen our understanding of its meaning. Jesus has been executed and his followers fear for their lives. At the very least, they feel as though they may have wasted years following this man who was now executed as a common criminal.

Even though they do not know him, the disciples walk with the stranger. When it is late, they invite him to stay with them. In this act of hospitality, the disciples demonstrate that they want to be a source of presence to the stranger. They dine together and then Jesus reveals himself in the breaking of the bread. After he vanishes, the disciples acknowledge that their hearts burned within them as Jesus spoke to them. Sometimes we wonder at the disciples for being foolish. How could they not recognize Jesus! But, I think they should be commended for their actions. Perhaps they did not recognize Jesus' form, but they followed his lead. Having seen him reach out to strangers like the crippled woman, they learned what it meant to act as Christ by extending the offer of fellowship and safety. If the stranger had traveled on alone, he could have been attacked on the road in the evening. The disciples recognized this and offered the stranger a place to rest and food for nourishment. The transformation was complete: they had been formed to be present to the needs of another.

We, too, can be transformed as the disciples were. We learn what it means to be present to others through moments when others are present to us, as well as through reading these Gospel narratives. The "others" that you encounter in homes and on the streets are working to transform you, just as you think your presence transforms them. This is the Spirit at work. The power of solidarity as a reciprocal moment of spiritual awakening is the work of the Gospel today. We honor those who teach us by bringing to others those lessons, those gifts, that presence. Even if sometimes we do not recognize what they have done until they vanish before our eyes.

Prayer and the Power of God

While any metaphor or idea of God falls far short of who and what God is, these images are important for the way we conduct our lives, especially in a time of service. In the previous chapter I mentioned the way Hauerwas interprets the use of prayer. It is important to say a bit more about prayer and what I think it can do, but also about ways in which I think prayer can be done in a harmful way that doesn't truly reflect its nature as communication with God. When I was a teenager, my uncle Richard contracted lung cancer. The disease swiftly took over his body. Despite aggressive chemotherapy, the cancer was unrelenting and he was moved to hospice after battling for about one year. I remember the last time I saw him. My parents and other relatives gathered around his bedside. One person asked if we could pray "over" my uncle. At this time, I was exploring religion and was still coming into my own understanding of what I believed about God. However, I remember clearly the opening words that were prayed as we held hands: "Lord Jesus, we know you could heal Uncle Richard if you wanted to . . ." At that point I lost focus and my mind wandered. *Is this true? If it is, then why isn't God doing something? Well, there must be a reason. . . .* I tuned back in for the *amen*, but then mentally retreated again. I remember saying goodbye to my uncle and knowing that would likely be the last time I would see him. On the ride home I kept wondering, *What divine reason is there for my uncle to be dying?* And, *If I were lying there dying, would I really want to hear people stand over me and say those words?*

Ultimately, the Catholic Church says suffering is a mystery. In chapter two we briefly touched on the man born blind in John 9. While the Pharisees thought the man was born blind because of the sins of his parents, the church rejects this view, as did Jesus. Job's friends, likewise, accuse him of deserving the punishments from God. This explanation is also rejected by the church. God does not

139

cause people to be sick as punishment for their actions. But this is only a partial answer to the question of my teenage mind. Okay, God did not make my uncle sick, but could God cure him, as suggested in the prayer? There have been countless books written on theodicy, the question of God's relationship to the problem of evil. I do not wish to enter into the debate from a philosophical level in this book, although I certainly encourage you to explore the question. Not because you will find the answer, but because how you see this question is very important to your time as a volunteer and for the rest of your life.

Instead of rehashing the arguments of theodicy, I want to reflect on a national bestseller *When Bad Things Happen to Good People* by Rabbi Harold Kushner. I believe this book is a bestseller because it speaks to the problem of evil in such a way that a person not trained in theology can nod and affirm, "Yes, that is my question too!" In exploring the text, I want to clearly delineate between theological doctrine and spirituality. While some of the theological assertions in Kushner's book run contrary to Catholic teaching, I think the spiritual avenue can be helpful for our prayer life and lead us closer toward, rather than away from, the Church's teachings on the mystery of suffering.

Kushner establishes his purpose for writing the book in its opening pages. His son passed away from a disease at a young age and Kushner was tormented by the "support" he received to explain why this happened. It is not that people meant to cause him pain. But hearing "It happened for a reason" or that it was God's plan to take his son away from him forced Kushner to reflect on what he thought about God, evil, and suffering. These reflections and musings became his book.

In the early chapters, Kushner rejects some of the traditional views on suffering. For example, suffering as punishment for things we did or will do, suffering as punishment for things our parents have done, suffering as a lesson to teach us something, and many other beliefs that rest the causality of suffering upon God's direct action or decision. But that begs an additional question: Could God prevent bad things? If God could, but chooses not to, isn't God morally liable?

An example I use in my class to explain this perspective is to imagine that I am sitting on my front porch. The porch is raised so I am above ground level. In this scenario I am talking to a student at the foot of the steps who then waves goodbye and walks toward the street. As he walks, he looks down at his phone and quickly becomes engrossed in a message. He continues to walk with his head down. There is a truck barreling down the road, and the driver is not paying attention. From my vantage point I see that the student isn't looking up and I see the driver speeding down the road. In three seconds my brain processes that the student is in danger and I have another few seconds where I could yell to the student to look up. However, I do not yell out or take any other action to prevent what becomes a horrible hit-and-run. My neighbor is watching through her upstairs window. Unfortunately, her window does not open so she could not yell down to warn the young man. She sees me watching the accident unfold and runs down to my porch. Bewildered, she chides me, "You watched it all happen and you could have prevented it! What kind of a person are you?" She would rightly be furious that I did nothing to prevent this suffering. I think any moral person would find at least some fault in the fact that I chose to do nothing. While this is a fictional example, I think it captures the predicament that Kushner articulates. Once we say God does not cause suffering, is it any greater benefit to say God could prevent tragedy, but chooses not to?

This fictional scenario leads us to Kushner's final chapter and his illumination of what he thinks is God's role in tragedy. He writes, "I believe in God. But I do not believe the same things about Him as I did years ago. . . . I recognize His limitations."[50] Kushner contends that God is limited by laws of nature and by human freedom. God does not stop human suffering because God is bound by the laws of nature and the gift of free will. Thus, in my previous example, God could not have warned the young man who was walking toward oncoming traffic without interfering with the laws of nature. God is still important and worthy of worship, however. Kushner explains, "God, who neither causes nor prevents tragedies, helps by inspiring people to help."[51] A flood that devastates a town is not caused by God, but those who rush to help others rebuild are inspired by God. Disease is similar. The COVID-19 pandemic was not sent from God as a punishment for

---

50. Harold Kushner, *When Bad Things Happen to Good People* (New York: Avon Books, 1981), 134.
51. Kushner, *Bad Things Happen*, 140.

humanity, but those who sat with the dying were inspired by the Spirit to bring presence at great risk to themselves.

While agreeing that God does not send plagues or illnesses like COVID-19, the Catholic Church disagrees with Kushner's conclusion that God has limitations. First, the church holds that God is immutable, changeless, and outside of time. Second, God is all-powerful and all-present. If we accept that the problem of suffering is ultimately a mystery and hold to the teachings of the church, I think we can still enlarge our perspective of the *image* of God to be the suffering presence described by Hauerwas. The God that Kushner rejects is the one who should be able to remove the binder of pain from our hands, while Hauerwas presents the God who holds up the binder from below. If we come to think of God as the suffering presence who is always present, instead of the one tasked with removing suffering from our lives, it may make it easier for us to accept the mystery of the suffering. This isn't a philosophical answer—it is a spiritual one. It does not address *why* bad things happen; rather, it understands God as the presence with us *when* they happen.

I began this section with a story on prayer. So, what to do with prayer? Is my Christian fundamentalist relative correct that God could have healed my uncle if "God wanted to"? I don't know. But I do know that when I am dying I do not want someone to hold over my head the unknown mystery of what God can do. I would much rather someone hold my hand and invite God into my life as a suffering presence. It is not for us to hold God's power over others like a trophy for the elect. Rather, we should swing wide the doors for God's love, the gift that desires to be spread. When we encounter the suffering of others, we should not "offer it up," but offer to take it on. Like Jesus, who placed his hands of love on the woman crippled by an evil spirit, we should not fear the retribution of the powerful for being a presence to the powerless. In that way, we lighten the load by taking one rock out of someone's bag.

Reflection Questions

1. Hospitality is a key component of being a suffering presence. Have you had an experience of hospitality, either receiving or giving, as the disciples did on the road to Emmaus?

2. What experiences of suffering have you observed daily in your immersion experience? Can you successfully delineate between suffering you can change and suffering you cannot?

3. What are your reactions to Kushner's "limitations of God"? Can you use his insights to inform your spirituality or relationship with God without accepting his theological conclusions?

Chapter 12

Gift of Self

In the final chapter of part four I would like to offer examples of Fr. Pedro Arrupe being a suffering presence and then invite you to prayerfully reflect on being a suffering presence to others during your time of service and in your life. Arrupe's experiences of accompaniment with those suffering are numerous. There are many stories just from his time in Hiroshima following the dropping of the atomic bomb. He witnessed horrible scenes and was powerless to save the thousands of people around him who were in agony following the blast.

One story that illustrates the power of being a suffering presence is his encounter with Nakamura, a young Japanese woman (the description of her wounds in this paragraph is graphic). She was a fervent Christian and received Communion every day at 6:30 a.m. Mass with Father Arrupe. As he was passing through the streets in the days following the bomb, he entered what was left of her home. There, lying on a table, was Nakamura. She was burned, and pus oozed from the sores on her body. She had been lying there for fifteen days, only moving to get rice for her wounded father. Her muscles were hollow and rotten as a mass of worms ate away at her insides. When Arrupe moved her, he put his hands on her back, but felt them push into her flesh. Her back was completely eaten away by radiation. As he put her down, she saw Arrupe and said only, "Father, have you brought me Communion?"[52] Arrupe brought her back to the novitiate and tried several procedures to save her life. He stayed by her bedside for several nights. After two months, she had a heart attack and died.[53] Arrupe had done all he could both medically and through his presence to save her life and make her comfortable.

Another example occurred when Arrupe, as superior general, visited Jesuits in Latin America. He was invited to offer Mass in a local slum. He found it difficult to say Mass, choking on his words as he realized how much these people loved Christ. Arrupe's homily was short and was more of a discourse with the people as they thanked him for sending Jesuits to offer Mass for them. He reflected, "At the consecration I elevated the Host and perceived in the absolute silence the joy of the Lord which is found among those who love him." While distributing Communion, Arrupe "noticed big tears like pearls on many of these faces, which were dry, hard, baked by the sun; they recognized Jesus, who was their only consolation. My hands trembled."[54]

52. Pedro Arrupe, S.J., *Recollections and Reflections of Pedro Arrupe, S.J.*, trans. Yolanda T. DeMola, S.C. (Wilmington, DE: Michael Glazier, 1986), 169.

53. Lamet, *Pedro Arrupe* 185–186.

54. Pedro Arrupe, S.J. *One Jesuit's Spiritual Journey: Autobiographical Conversations with Claude Dietsch, S.J.* trans. Ruth Bradley (St. Louis, MO: The Institute of Jesuit Sources, 1986), 35.

After Mass a man approached Arrupe and told him he wanted to show him something at his house. Arrupe was hesitant to go with him, but another Jesuit encouraged him and told him that he would be in no danger because the people were good and kind. Arrupe entered the man's house, a structure that was barely standing. The host offered him a rickety chair and asked him to sit down. A short time later, the sun began to set. The two sat in silence for several minutes. The man then said, "I didn't know how I would thank you for all you have done for us. I have nothing to give you, but I thought you would like to see this sunset."[55]

Some may argue that sitting with a poor man in a chair watching the sunset is not an action of justice. On the surface, it was a small amount of time that Arrupe spent with the man in his house. Arrupe didn't know much about this man or his life and struggles. He knew he lived in a difficult area and was materially poor. But he trusted that his presence would make a difference. This is a beautiful example of Arrupe not trying to do too much. He isn't trying to solve the man's problems. He is sitting with him in those problems, literally. And he was rewarded with the only gift the man could give—a glimpse of the beauty of God's creation. The presence Arrupe gave to the man became a gift for them both.

---

55. Arrupe, *Spiritual Journey*, 36.

Inviting God

During in-country retreats for the *Rostro de Cristo* volunteers, I invite them to reflect on the reality of the suffering they observed while living in Ecuador. I hope this exercise offers them a space to reflect on the suffering of those neighbors they have come to love and a way to bring that suffering to God. I ask the volunteers to compile a list of people whom they wish to pray for, followed by a sentence describing the needs of that person. For example, "For Jose, who is preparing to begin at a new school" or "For Maria, who is abused by her husband." Then, in the evening, we gather together around a candle or fire and prayerfully offer these intentions to God. It is often an emotional experience to hear a loved one's name and to know a sense of powerlessness in fighting against their struggles.

When I developed this exercise I hoped for at least one of three things: First, I hoped that it would bring the volunteer community together to sit with the reality of the suffering of people who are loved. Second, I believe that suffering loses power when it is unmasked. Evil that is latent can thrive more readily than when it is known and when burdens are shared. And third, although I do not expect God to suddenly heal each of these people, I do believe there is something theologically significant in bringing these people before God. It is not something I can explain, but something about the mysterious reality of God's love. It is not that God did not know of these injustices before they were named, but that in naming them, we invite God anew into the unfolding drama of the lives of those who suffer injustice.

Reflection Questions

1. Have you had an experience in your time of service when you moved to judgment, like Arrupe in the Latin American village, but ultimately became a suffering presence to others without meaning to?

2. Take time to list, by name if possible, the people you have encountered during your time of service and their experience of suffering. Pray for them with your community. Lift them up to the God of love who knows each of them by name.

Conclusion

Limits to Being a Suffering Presence

There are, of course, limits to the idea of being a suffering presence. This concept is not meant to answer all questions of how to deal with any pain and injustice that you witness in your locations. I think these limitations are important to raise at this time. First, this method presupposes that the other person invites or welcomes you to sit with them. What if this is not the case and your offer is rejected, or, at the very least, not realized?

In some cases, a person may not want someone to be present. Growing up I had a friend who was like a younger brother. Mike, or as I nicknamed him, Mac, was two years younger than me. We lived near each other and spent countless hours together. We attended separate colleges two hours apart, but we still got together as often as possible. A few years after Mac graduated I noticed some changes in his personality. Our chances to get together became less frequent and when we did meet up, he would withdraw and sometimes act out in anger in ways I had not seen before. One day, he called to tell me he had quit his job and that he knew people were following him. He said he was going to get even with "those people" and hung up. What followed were months of worrying for his safety as his sister, his parents, and I worked to get him the help he needed. He began taking medication that would sometimes help him with his delusions, but at other times they returned. The last time he came to visit me, he told me in the morning that it is scary when you think someone is following you, but you know it isn't true. Just a few hours later, he told me that he would "find out who it is and they would be sorry." Over the course of that day he had gone from being aware of his condition to falling back into it. These changes could be rapid and it was difficult for me to know what to say to help him. Less than a month later, he took his own life.

I share this story because it is a story of helplessness. I do not blame myself for Mac's decision to end his life. I do wish I had been able to figure out how to be more present to him. That isn't guilt; it's my realization that I am woefully ill-equipped to know how to accompany my friends who suffer from mental illness, depression, or schizophrenia. It was easier for me to sit silently with Dragan after his father's stroke than it was for me to argue with Mac, begging him to allow me to be present as he continually pushed me away. Not everyone will accept your invitation to be present. That doesn't mean you have failed, even if it feels that way.

Second, taking on the burden of the other can be draining and debilitating. Sometimes, when you remove a rock from the bag of another person, parts of it chip off into yours, and eventually your bag is made heavier through the process of being a suffering presence. The importance of self-care cannot be overstated. Hopefully, you have a community to help process this time. Being "successful" as a suffering presence (however you wish to define that) is difficult enough, but when you are pushed away continually, it can become damaging. It may mean that you have to get more creative with ways to offer presence, such as inviting others who have more experience into the circle of compassion, or, like in Mac's case, encouraging them to seek professional care.

The suffering presence approach has limits, but it can also be an important method, especially for those who are doing a short-term immersion trip. There isn't time to do much else. The idea of being a suffering presence isn't applicable to every situation of suffering you will face. It is, however, one method of service. It is one tool that you can utilize when trying to lighten the load of another. While it may not explain the mystery of why people suffer, bearing some of the load for another can make a difference. So, as you navigate the injustices around you, take time to sit in a chair and view the sunset with someone who is lonely. Reach into the bag and lighten the load of another traveler. You may find your own bag lighter as you stand to go your separate ways. In that mutual giving of presence, you may discover the God who calls to each of us by name.

Part Five

Does Anyone Know
What I Am Going Through?

During my early days of participating in immersion programs I told students that it was important to live simply, so we could be in solidarity with the people we would encounter. My first immersion was to Louisville, Kentucky, where John Carroll students and I worked with refugees. We learned about the difficulties of being a refugee in the United States and spent the week tutoring adults and playing with children. A year later I was the faculty member for a trip to Immokalee, Florida. Here, the students slept on the floor of a gym as we spent the days learning about immigration law and the rights of farmworkers. I thought we were denying ourselves the usual comforts—a bed, showers, privacy, and the food of our choice—so we could be in solidarity with people who slept in crowded trailers and/or had little access to water. Solidarity, to me, meant that we were "like them" for the week and that this experience would give us an insight into what it meant to be a refugee or an immigrant.

In sharing these perspectives, I have to again remind myself of my own advice from part one. The *Spirituality of Imperfection* cautions me to tread lightly on past views and experiences that made sense at the time, but may now seem problematic. While I can still acknowledge the importance of efforts and motivations to live simply while participating in these experiences, I find that using the word "solidarity" to describe what we were doing is spurious. There are many comprehensive books written on the historical development of the term "solidarity," so I will not rehash those discussions here. Rather, in chapter thirteen I hope to offer a few perspectives on solidarity that are helpful for wrestling with this concept. These reflections will begin with a homily by Pope Francis and then explore the workers in the vineyard parable in Matthew 20. In chapter fourteen, we will examine Pedro Arrupe's experiences in Japan for what they can teach about solidarity as lived out in immersion work. Finally, we will conclude part five with an invitation for you to decide for yourself if solidarity is even a possible goal for your immersion experience, whatever its length may be.

Chapter 13

Solidarity at Lampedusa

In July 2013 I was preparing to give a presentation on Ignatian spirituality at the *Rostro de Cristo* and Jesuit Volunteer International orientation program at the University of Scranton. The night before the presentation I received an email from a friend containing a link to one of Pope Francis's homilies. Francis had been elected only a few months prior, and although there was a sense of interest from Jesuit circles, there was also uncertainty about the "way of proceeding" with this "Jesuit Pope." I opened the link and read the homily. I then looked up from my laptop astonished that Pope Francis had just rewritten the core message of my talk.

One of the first places Pope Francis traveled after becoming pope was Lampedusa, an Italian island in the Mediterranean Sea where many refugees flee for safety and an opportunity for work. They travel from the eastern coast of Africa, risking their lives on unsafe boats. The link that had been emailed to me was the homily Pope Francis gave on the island. Francis begins by remarking that these ships should be vehicles of hope but end up being vehicles of death.

Francis recalls the questions of God to Adam and to Cain in Genesis. To Adam, God asked, "Where are you?" and to Cain he asked, "Where is your brother?" Both of these questions invite the addressee to realize they have lost their way. Adam was hiding from God because he knew he had sinned, while Cain hid because he had killed his brother. Francis says we, too, have lost our bearings. Like Abel's, the blood of those we discard cries out for justice. Who is responsible for the situation that causes people to be forgotten and marginalized? Francis says we are all responsible. Yet, when asked, we deny our responsibility for the situation. The pope explains, "The culture of comfort, which makes us think of only ourselves, makes us insensitive to the cries of other people, . . . it even leads to the globalization of indifference."[56] The globalization of indifference became a central theme in Francis's apostolic exhortation *Evangelii Gaudium*, which was released later that year.

The conclusion of the homily challenges people to a new understanding of solidarity. Francis asks if anyone in society has wept for the death of these people today. He then remarks, "We are a society that has forgotten how to weep, how to experience compassion—'suffering with' others."[57] Most who read this homily would agree with Francis's contention that we have not "wept for these people," because

---

56. Pope Francis, "*Homily of the Holy Father*," July 8, 2013, www.vatican. va/content/francesco/en/homilies/2013/documents/papa-frances-co_20130708_omelia-lampedusa.html.

57. Francis, "*Homily of the Holy Father*."

most have never heard of Lampedusa. Even those who have, if they are not directly related to this place or these people, simply dismiss it as unfortunate news. But Francis says it is not enough to know of it or to be moved for the moment. We need to make the plight of the "boat people" our plight. Solidarity, as Francis envisions it, is not the words of "we are all in this together," but the actions that result from this realization.

Taking these concepts a step further in *Evangelii Gaudium*, Francis offers a critique of previous perspectives on solidarity. He explains, "The word 'solidarity' is a little worn and at times poorly understood, but it refers to something more than a few sporadic acts of generosity. It presumes the creation of a new mindset which thinks in terms of community and the priority of the life of all over the appropriation of goods by a few."[58] This new mindset, one of the central insights of the exhortation, challenges people to see their decisions, not in terms of what can benefit themselves, but for how they affect all people. The common good should be served by the decisions of those in power. Private property is important, but should not usurp the needs of the community. A powerful image in *Evangelii Gaudium* is found in paragraph 53 where Francis ponders, "How can it be that it is not a news item when an elderly homeless person dies of exposure, but it is news when the stock market loses two points?"[59] If he were revising this

58. Francis, *Evangelii Gaudium: On the Proclamation of the Gospel in Today's World*, November 24, 2013, paragraph 188.
59. Francis, *Evangelii Gaudium* paragraph 53.

statement for 2020, Francis would likely highlight how many in society see the victims of COVID-19 as numbers, rather than as human individuals. Or, in the United States especially, how we need to see the victims of racial injustice not as numbers, but individuals with unique identities. The news of every death should cause us to weep. Solidarity demands a more in-depth understanding of the plight of others, because, in the end, it is our plight as well.

Care for the Workers in the Vineyard

The radical care that Francis describes in his homily at Lampedusa and in *Evangelii Gaudium* has its roots in the Gospel. Maria Riley, OP, discusses the importance of solidarity in Jesus' mission when she writes, "Jesus' journey towards Calvary was not a journey toward self-sacrifice so much as it was a journey of radical acts of love that deepened relationships, embodied and extended community, and passed on the gift of life."[60] As Christians, we are called to embody this gift of life that Jesus offered in his death and to carry the transformative elements of solidarity in our hearts. Riley concludes, "Solidarity is first of all an experi-

---

60. Maria Riley, O.P., "Feminist Analysis: A Missing Perspective," in *The Logic of Solidarity: Commentaries on Pope John Paul II's Encyclical 'On Social Concern'*. ed. Gregory Baum and Robert Ellsberg (Maryknoll, New York: Orbis Books, 1989), 199.

ence of relationship, rather than an abstract virtue."[61] The importance of relationship is exemplified by the numerous Gospel accounts of Jesus eating with those discarded or conversing with those seen as unclean.

One parable that illustrates solidarity and care for others is sometimes dismissed as foolish sophistry. The parable of the workers in the vineyard, found in Matthew 20, is a story that my father, a small business owner, once told me was the "reason he stopped going to church." Although he was being facetious, he is correct that it is often misunderstood and sounds ridiculous without context.

Jesus begins the parable with his phrase, "The kingdom of heaven is like . . ." which clues us in that the way people are treated in the parable gives us a glimpse into the way people will be treated in heaven, the archetype of how we should strive to treat others in this life. Jesus proceeds to tell the story of a landowner who hires workers for his vineyard. The landowner goes out "early" and agrees to pay these workers the regular day's wage. He then goes out at 9:00, 12:00, 3:00, and 5:00. Each time, he sees people and asks if someone has hired them, and they reply "no." And each time he tells them he will pay them a fair wage. At the end of the workday, the landowner tells the foreman to pay everyone, starting with those who arrived last. To the surprise of those who were hired earlier, all are given the same wage. Those who worked the longest are angry at the landowner, but he tells them, "Am I not allowed to do

---

61. Riley, "Feminist Analysis," 199.

what I choose with what belongs to me? Or are you envious because I am generous?" (Mt 20:1–16).

Homilies preached on this passage often focus on the generosity of God. Sometimes, I have heard a preacher focus on the realization that God can forgive all people through God's love, which is symbolized by the daily wage. I do not think these are "wrong" interpretations, but they have little connection to how I should live my life. God is certainly generous with God's gifts, and God can do whatever God wants with our "daily wage." But perhaps this passage means something else too.

During Ignatian Heritage Week at John Carroll University in 2018 I heard Jesuit scholar Fr. Mark Ravizza share his interpretation of the parable. It captures something that I had never considered about its meaning. Father Ravizza asked us to key in on a few crucial details in order to offer a different perspective that applies to how we are to understand the landowner and to our role in understanding others. Using the imagination, as discussed in part one, we can envision the scene playing out in our minds so we can go deeper into its meaning. First, the landowner is the one going back and forth to the town to hire the workers. This is odd, as he should have had others to do this work for him. Thus, there is some reason that Jesus points out that the landowner is doing this menial task. Second, the landowner specifically asks why the people are still waiting, to which they reply that no one has hired them. Third, when they pay the workers, the landowner asks the foreman to first pay those who worked the least. He would have known that paying the people who worked the longest last would allow them to see that all the workers are being paid the same. If he had the longest-working group paid first, they would have left right away. They never would have known what the others were paid. Thus, there must be significance to the order, as the landowner should have known people would be upset with him for the perceived "disparity" in payment.

After pointing out these details, Father Ravizza explained how he understood the parable. The landowner went to the town because he wanted to see if the others had been given the opportunity to work. Each time, he saw people who wanted to work but had not been hired. He knew that if he did not hire them, they would not get work for the day, especially those hired at the end of the day. It is not that they were lazy. They waited and no one hired them. His choice to pay the most recent workers first was not a mistake; it was intended to demonstrate his care for those workers through his generosity. Generosity is not the focus, but it is the vehicle for justice. The landowner knows that if they are not paid a full wage they will not have enough money to eat. It is not the workers' fault they were not picked earlier. And so, the landowner is shocked at the outrage of the workers who feel they are being cheated. It is his money to do with as he pleases, but justice and solidarity demand that he take care of everyone. It is not a question of who is deserving. All people deserve to have enough money to eat.

Father Ravizza then connected the movements of this passage to the Filipino word *kapwa*. Although it lacks a direct translation to English, he said it embodies what we see in this passage: the giving of self so others can have enough to eat. He then concluded that justice is "about God being made whole." God is made whole when all are invited to the table. During the question-and-answer session, he said that the closest word to translate *kapwa* would be "kinship": a sense of connection that is like a familial relationship and also denotes a deep care for others.

The visual of people lining up to work and waiting to be selected made me immediately think of the migrant workers in Immokalee, Florida. In Immokalee, workers line up in the parking lot, waiting to be chosen to go to the fields. Those who are not selected could wait all day hoping for other work. If they do not work that day, they do not get paid. During one of my trips to Immokalee to introduce university students to the realities of immigration and the plight of migrant farmworkers, I had the opportunity to meet with one of my personal heroes, Gerardo Reyes Chavez, who is a member of the Coalition of Immokalee Workers. I had been to Immokalee many times, but usually during spring break, when he was leading a protest on behalf of the farmworkers. So, when I finally got to meet him and hear his presentation it was a true gift. His wisdom and way of articulating the plight of farmworkers gave me goosebumps. One of the students asked him, "How can we make a difference, beyond boycotts and protesting with the farmworkers?" He thought for a moment and then replied, "When you talk about us, talk about us as you would a friend." It was so simple, yet powerful. He was describing solidarity. He doesn't want a handout any more than the workers in the vineyard. Because in friendship, in *kapwa*, we weep for the plight of the migrants, we weep for the boat people of Lampedusa, we weep for ourselves because we know that God must be made whole.

Reflection Questions

1. Is it possible to live in the world the way Pope Francis advocates in his homily at Lampedusa? Should we weep every time a person suffers a tragedy?

2. Do you agree with Father Ravizza's interpretation of the parable of the workers in the vineyard? If he is correct, what implications does this interpretation have for the way we treat those who are unable to work?

Chapter 14

Solidarity as Kinship

In Jesuit circles, the use of the word *kinship* often calls to mind the work of Fr. Greg Boyle. Boyle is a Jesuit priest who founded a gang-intervention youth program called Homeboy Industries to help former gang members get jobs and gain skills to help them after time in prison. His work with Homeboy Industries has been well documented. He travels the country and gives over two hundred talks a year at universities, churches, retreats, and other public engagements. His message is told through stories of working with the "homies," as he refers to the former gang members. Boyle's work has changed not only the lives of these men and women, but also the lives of those who hear his words and his stories. As Pope Francis gives us a macro-level view of solidarity at Lampedusa, and parable of the workers in the vineyard gives us a scriptural interpretation, Father Boyle's experience offers us a specific example of these perspectives in action.

The word Boyle uses for solidarity in his speeches and writings is *kinship*. To explain kinship, he states: "Kinship—not serving the other, but being one with the other. Jesus was not 'a man for others'; he was one with them. There is a world of difference in that."[62] Many Ignatian documents talk of "serving the poor" and being a woman or man for others, but Boyle points out a dimension of solidarity (or kinship) that goes beyond service and being "for others." While service is a start, it is not the end product if a relationship of solidarity exists. There should not be an "us" and a "them," but only an "us." He hypothesizes, "Often we strike the high moral distance that separates 'us' from 'them,' and yet, it is God's dream come true when we recognize that there exists no daylight between us. Serving others is good, it's a start. But it's just the hallway that leads to the Grand Ballroom."[63] Seeing the other as someone in need of service or charity never allows the relationship to develop into kinship, or as Boyle states, what God had in mind.

The challenge to embodying kinship is that the population that Boyle works with is often despised or feared by the general public. Gang members, covered in tattoos and with criminal records, may invoke pity, but rarely a sense of kinship. But kinship requires a push beyond the surface, beyond the crimes of the past, to seeing the person's worth and full dignity. The farther out into the margins someone is, the harder it is to create kinship with them. Boyle offers, "Soon we imagine, with God, this circle of compassion. Then we imagine no one standing outside of that circle, moving ourselves closer to the margins so that the margins will be erased.

---

62. Greg Boyle, S.J., *Tattoos on the Heart: The Power of Boundless Compassion* (New York: Free Press, 2010), 188.
63. Boyle, *Tattoos*, 188.

We stand there with those whose dignity has been denied . . . with the demonized so the demonizing will stop."[64]

One story from his book *Tattoos on the Heart* begins with a trip Boyle took to the White House with three "homies." On the flight home, one member of the group went to the restroom, but did not return for forty-five minutes. When he finally sat down, Boyle inquired what took him so long. The homie, named Alex, said he was talking to the flight attendant. He sheepishly added, "I made her cry. I hope that's okay."[65] Boyle, perhaps fearing the worst, told him that might depend on what he said to her. Alex then explained how she asked him about his tattoos and gang life and that he told her all about Homeboy Industries and their trip to the White House. This is what caused her to cry. Boyle replied, "Well, mijo, whaddya 'spect? She just caught a glimpse of ya. She saw that you were somebody. She recognized you . . . as the shape of God's heart. Sometimes people cry when they see that."[66]

Boyle sees in this interaction, this exchange between two people, kinship. The flight attendant who was curious enough to ask this "dangerous"-looking, tattoo-covered former gang member about his life, and in return his willingness to share his life with a total stranger, created a space for connection. Boyle insightfully concludes, "Suddenly, kinship—two souls feeling their worth, flight attendant, gang member, 34,000 feet—no daylight separating them. Exactly

---

64. Boyle, *Tattoos*, 190.
65. Boyle, *Tattoos*, 204.
66. Boyle, *Tattoos*, 205.

what God had in mind."[67] After this encounter, both see the other differently, as people, worthy of a new level of care and respect. A relationship had formed from the vulnerability of one and the interest of the other. Within that exchange, kinship grew as there was no longer an "us" and a "them," but only an "us." Therein lies an expression of *kapwa*. God is made whole when the circle of compassion is enlarged so that all can fit, even those who stand waiting to be chosen for the right to work and the right to be seen as an equal.

Learning the Soul

Thus far, the concept of solidarity has been addressed on the level of human beings encountering others and realizing that the things that make us alike are far more numerous than what keeps us separate. We see this in the Lampedusa homily, as solidarity calls us to weep for those whom we do not know personally. We see this in the vineyard parable, where we are responsible for other human beings so that all may be able to eat. And we see from Father Boyle that the distance between us and others shouldn't keep us from caring for them. There is another important element to consider, one which Pedro Arrupe had specific experience in overcoming. How does one create solidarity when separated by culture, language, or religion? During his time as

---

67. Boyle, *Tattoos*, 205.

a missionary in Japan, Arrupe sought to bring Christianity to the Japanese in a way that was peaceful, honest, and authentic. His experiences will hopefully be helpful as you learn a new culture or way of life and attempt to create a sense of solidarity with those whom you encounter or with whom you share community.

Early in his Jesuit training, Arrupe wanted to go to Japan to be a missionary in the footsteps of Francis Xavier. In 1938, while in the United States, he received a letter from the superior general, telling him that his request to be sent to Japan had been approved. Early on, Arrupe struggled to learn Japanese, despite his background in languages. He also suffered from "culture shock" as he attempted to learn Japanese customs. However, as George Bishop, a biographer of Arrupe, points out, "Without assimilating the culture and without speaking the language there was no possibility of preaching Christianity."[68] During his time in Yamaguchi, Arrupe slowly began to win the hearts of the people. As Robert Rush, a good friend of Arrupe's later in life, reflected, "His missionary activities were sometimes unique. The most extraordinary, perhaps, was the use of the concerts he gave. . . . It was a case of anything that would help to make Christ and his Church better known."[69]

On March 9, 1942, Father Lasalle, the superior, asked Arrupe if he would like to go to Hiroshima to become the novice master because the current one was very ill. As novice master, Arrupe knew he had to know more than the Japanese

---

68. Bishop, *Pedro Arrupe*, 8.
69. Bishop, *Pedro Arrupe*, 8.

language to work with the novices and to be accepted. Bishop states, "He would have to know and appreciate their culture. He became obsessed with knowing all about Japanese people and culture from the inside."[70] Another biographer, Hedwig Lewis, offers some examples of the way Arrupe sought to learn more about the Japanese, citing a statement from Arrupe concerning his approach in Japan:

> Which paths [of inculturation] was I to follow to reach the Japanese soul? The paths (do) of Zen. In other words, the manner of serving tea (chado) . . . the manner of shooting with a bow (kyodo) . . . the manner of arranging a bouquet of flowers (kado) . . . the manner of defending oneself (judo) . . . fencing (kendo). . . . And finally (shodo) the way in which a poem is composed and written.[71]

Overall, Arrupe reflects: "To sum up, I would say: If a man truly wishes to work with a people, he must understand the soul of that people."[72] Within this insight, solidarity through inculturation is exemplified. To work with others, to enter into a relationship of solidarity, a person should work to understand the soul of the other. This does not mean that you truly become another race, religion, or nationality. Arrupe was always a Spanish Basque man.

---

70. Bishop, *Pedro Arrupe*, 85.
71. Lewis, *Arrupe Treasury*, 33.
72. Lewis, *Arrupe Treasury*, 33.

But in working with the Japanese, he honored and learned their customs and treasured them as his own. In this way he gained their trust and admiration and learned much for himself about life and etiquette from his Japanese teachers.

Within a few days of his arrival, Arrupe sought out a teacher to instruct him in the tea ceremony. In Zen Buddhism, the tea ceremony was "one of the means of getting insight into one's inner soul."[73] Knowing the importance of this ceremony in Japanese culture, Arrupe worked diligently to understand it. One day, he asked his instructor how long it would be until he could lead the ritual. The instructor replied that in three years he might be qualified.[74] For Arrupe, acquiring this knowledge wasn't a matter of mastering skill or technique, but a way into the soul, the essence of what it meant to be Japanese. Studying culture is not a surface-level demonstration or performance, but allows one to get to the heart of what makes people different and attempts to appropriately integrate these differences into one's own life.

While Arrupe's efforts sound authentic, their success lies in the responses he received from Jesuits and from those who converted because of his efforts. One example of the way he touched the lives of the Japanese during his time as novice director involved a young man named Jo Hayazoe, who joined the novitiate under his guidance.[75] He assisted Arrupe with catechism classes. One day he

73. Bishop, *Pedro Arrupe*, 85.
74. Bishop, *Pedro Arrupe*, 86.
75. Bishop, *Pedro Arrupe*, 88.

asked an old Japanese man who attended these classes if he understood what was being said by the priest. The old man replied that he was deaf, but that he had been looking into Arrupe's eyes every day and that his eyes convinced him that Arrupe's lessons were true. "What he believes, I believe," replied the old man.[76]

Years later, Father Hayazoe reflected that Arrupe was the model of a Japanese saint. He was humble and never angry at those who sought him out. Other novices would comment on how he was personable to each of them. They said, "He knew each novice personally and treated each individually, adapting his approach according to different circumstances and personalities. He would often ask forgiveness of his students."[77] Arrupe would also do tasks usually reserved for "lower" classes in society, such as cleaning the novices' shoes and cleaning the sewage system. Arrupe passed the importance of humility on to the novices as well, by having them walk behind horses to collect their dung with a bucket.

These stories about Arrupe offer important insights for our understanding of solidarity, as well as ways to grapple with this concept during immersion work. First, there is Arrupe's beautiful articulation of "learning the soul" of another. There is no concrete method for doing this that works in all cases. But, I think Arrupe's examples with the tea ceremony, fencing, judo, and other practices all show Arrupe engaging with the icons of another culture. Second,

---

76. Bishop, *Pedro Arrupe*, 89.
77. Bishop, *Pedro Arrupe*, 89.

he is not doing it individually, but through the tutelage of others. This naturally leads us to the importance of invitation. To grow in solidarity with another, especially during immersion work, means to ask to learn from another. This humility explains the elderly man's observation that he learned by watching Arrupe and looking into his eyes. And third, Arrupe teaches us to learn as much as we can about an individual. While inculturation requires one to take on the culture, accompaniment of an individual should always take precedence. Even as superior general, Arrupe visited as many Jesuit houses as he could all over the world. Each person knew that he cared for them as individuals. With these three ideas in tandem—the soul of a culture, the humility of the approach, and the care for the individual—we now turn to a model for growing in solidarity and the importance of immersion work for this process.

Reflection Questions

1. Do you have an experience of kinship in your life that is not connected to service? Revisit that experience and journal about it. What elements of that relationship can you try to bring to your service experience?

2. Arrupe sought to learn the customs and ways of the Japanese people, both before his assignment in Japan and during his time there. In what ways have you or your immersion program or community attempted to "learn the soul" of the people as Arrupe did?

Chapter 15

The Asymptote

There are not many things I remember from high school math. I struggled to get Cs, especially in algebra and algebra II. So, when a family friend told me that the way I was describing Arrupe's experiences of solidarity sounded like a curve approaching an asymptote, I was intrigued. It was the summer of 2012 and I was trying to get a handle on my dissertation research, which focused on Arrupe and solidarity. This image gave me the conceptual framework I needed to pull my ideas together. In this chapter I want to explain what an asymptote is and why I think it is a crucial image for your time of service.

An asymptote is a line that a given curve continually approaches but does not meet at any finite distance. As the curve approaches infinity, it gets closer and closer to the asymptote, but will never touch it. This analogy highlights three important insights about solidarity. First, in solidarity, like the lines that will never meet, you will never become the other person. Second, just as the curve goes on for infinity, solidarity is an ongoing process that is never completed. And third, the functions that describe a line curving toward an asymptote are varied—they do not all look the same.

Thus, the framework for solidarity must be personalized, rather than providing a cookie-cutter model that applies to everyone in the same way. These insights are not only important for service work, but for an understanding of relationships with friends and family as we move closer to the other person, if given the invitation and opportunity.

The first insight is important for retaining one's individuality. Arrupe never became Japanese. He always remained himself, even though he lived in Japan for twenty-five years, learned the language, and learned many Japanese customs. We can never become anything other than ourselves. There will always be things that keep you from being the other. When I first began working with *Rostro de Cristo*, a few years before I visited Ecuador, I asked a former volunteer about the idea of solidarity and what it meant to live in solidarity with Ecuadorians. She pulled out her passport and showed it to me. "As long as I have this, I won't be like many of the neighbors who could never come to the United States." It was a simple yet powerful insight. As a white male from the United States, I will always be afforded privileges that are denied to women, people of color, or immigrants. This was one of the earliest moments that I realized the privilege of my whiteness. The asymptote reminds me that my privilege is not something I can give away, nor something I can shed when I want to be more "like" another person. As someone who has decided to enter into the community of another, always remember that some form of privilege is part of who you are, simply by the fact that you are able to *choose* to be present in that place while others may not have that choice.

The second insight is that solidarity is a process and not an end product. Since coming to this understanding, I have tried to not speak of being "in" solidarity with someone, but rather of "growing toward" solidarity with someone. As a first-year student at John Carroll University I read *The Tortilla Curtain* by T. C. Boyle. I remember being moved by the reality of what it means to live as an undocumented immigrant, but I didn't *really* know what that meant. Eventually, I heard fellow students speak about immersion trips where they met undocumented persons. It was still hard for me to conceptualize. Eventually, I met people in these places myself. Then, over time, I became friends with people and learned about their lives, not as a college student reading a book, but as a human being welcoming people inside the circle of compassion. I now weep, not because of the abstract concept of people being unjustly discriminated against, but because these people are my friends. But I have a long way to go in this process and I hope to continue to grow toward solidarity with others who experience oppression, marginalization, and discrimination.

And finally, this method of understanding solidarity is different for different people. In the first story of part five I recalled a time when I thought that not showering brought my students and me into solidarity with migrant workers. I added that such an action can have value, but we are fooling ourselves if we think that puts us in solidarity with other people. I think the best way to describe that particular action is to say it is a small movement toward the asymptote of solidarity. For a student who had no idea what it is like to have to shower with a hose for a week, this could be a powerful realization that not everyone in the world has access to unlimited water. This sounds trivial and demeaning to those who understand that not showering has nothing to do with encountering a farmworker who experiences poverty from an unjust social system and inhumane immigration policies. For a person much further along the curve, at a place where solidarity is greater, it may seem insulting. But gently working with people as they discover the world is important for justice work as well. We teach people about the reality of life for others and invite them to continue to integrate that discovery into their own lives. That is what it means to see solidarity as an *individual* process.

I hope this model is helpful for reflecting on your solidarity with those in your service community. At its heart is my belief that one of the worst things you can say to a person is, "I know what you are going through." We never know what someone else is going through. We might have had similar experiences, but the way those experiences impact me can be very different from the way they impact you. Because I have been through a breakup does not mean I should attempt to help someone else through one by assuming that I know what he or she is going through. Even identical twins never know everything about what the other is "going through," so how can we assume this about our friends or those we meet during a time of service? While a statement like this usually comes from a place of care, it likely ends in a place of hurt. The curve and the asymptote never touch. The best we can do is hope to be invited to grow closer to the line of another.

Reflection Questions

1. Draw the curve of solidarity for your experiences. Label moments that have slowly brought you closer to the point where you are now, in terms of understanding an injustice or something you have encountered during your time of service.

2. What elements of culture, such as customs, language, and traditions, would best allow you to grow toward solidarity with the people you will encounter in your service experience?

Conclusion

Solidarity in Graced Moments

My friend Lisa became a second mother to me when I lived with her, her husband, and their daughter for five years during my doctoral studies. In March 2018 I saw her for the last time. She had been diagnosed with an aggressive form of ovarian cancer. I was greeted at the door by her husband, Paul, who told me that she had not been doing well and was very weak. I sat at her bedside and we spoke about traveling and other things, making small talk. After about an hour I could tell she was getting tired so I stood to depart. I put my hand on her shoulder and told her, "You have been my inspiration." She immediately responded, "And you have been mine." Somehow, I kept my composure in the moment, but tears filled my eyes when I got back to my car. I can only describe that moment, that interaction, as one of graced solidarity.

It had been Lisa who, six months earlier, had encouraged me to travel to Tanzania for the Jesuit Volunteer Corps to lead the retreat. I told her about my fears of getting sick, how cystic fibrosis constantly instilled fear in me about not being able to do my daily treatments or becoming ill. Despite all my healthy trips to Ecuador,

I couldn't get around the fact that Tanzania was farther away. But Lisa, who had been fighting to stay alive, reminded me how important it is to experience life and to live it while I can. After fighting cancer and watching it take away her opportunities to travel, she wanted me to travel while I could. Lisa knew a lot about CF and had always pushed me to take risks. She said I had inspired her with the way I lived my life, and now, she was inspiring me. That graced moment the last time we saw each other was a moment of solidarity. I can't explain it, but I felt it. I didn't know what she was going through, but I knew that I was inspired by it and that our struggles to survive had a similarity. From that similarity, we each drew strength. It was a realization that we both knew what it meant to live with a debilitating condition.

During your work of service, you will hopefully grow closer to those you accompany. This looks different for each person and in each place. But I hope that these reflections have given you new perspectives to consider in your time of accompaniment and movement toward what it means to live in a process of solidarity. It is important to be a person with others, not for others. "With" is the language of solidarity, a dialect of kinship. In the Kingdom of God there are no outcasts because we all have the same value. It is the place where God is made whole because we all weep for the discarded, not because they are discarded, but because we come to see them, and talk about them, as a friend.

Part Six

Honoring Your Experience

I spent ten days in Honduras in 2013 with a group of John Carroll students. The trip was organized by Hope for Honduran Children, a nonprofit that partnered with the John Carroll Boler College of Business. One day we traveled to a village in the mountains. As our bus ascended from the foot of the mountain we came upon a man walking with a backpack. The leaders of our trip, Karen and John, asked the bus driver to pull over. They invited the man to join us and explained that he was the teacher at the rural school we were preparing to visit. I later learned that this man's name was Moncho and that he lived at the base of the mountain. Five days a week he walked more than two hours to school, taught the young students for a few hours, and then walked back to his home. He had not been paid in over six months. We were shocked at his dedication to his students, despite the injustice he suffered in not being paid for his work. At the school we met his students and spent the morning with them.

As we were leaving, one of the members of our group asked Moncho why he was so driven to help the children.

He reflected for a moment and then told us that most of these children would never get jobs because employment opportunities in their villages were nearly nonexistent. However, a few months before, he was in a store in Tegucigalpa, the capital of Honduras, and the clerk who waited on him was one of his former students. With a smile on his face, Moncho told us that that is the reason he is so driven. The possibility that one of his students could escape poverty and get a job gave him the energy to continue. If just one student could make it and have a chance to earn a living, all of his work was worth it. As we rode the bus back to the community where we were staying I could not stop thinking about his dedication. I was a month away from defending my dissertation and applying for teaching jobs. I vowed to honor Moncho's example by striving to put the needs of my students before financial considerations or other restrictions. He is my exemplar of what it means to be a *profesor*, a teacher.

Part six will offer ideas for how you can make sense of an immersion or postgraduate volunteer experience. Perhaps even more so than the other concepts in this book, honoring your experience is an individual event. Even though your group or community shared an experience, what it means for the rest of your life can be quite subjective. While I can assume that Moncho's story continues to inspire others from our group, it is likely that they would point to different conversations or encounters from our time in Honduras as the most formative for them. This is not an area that should be forced. No one else can interpret what an experience means to you. I encourage you to continue having conversations with others and bringing service experiences to your prayer. Uncovering the meaning of an experience can take a long time, and what it means to you will likely change over time.

Part six concludes this book by offering you a variety of ways to honor your service experiences. Chapter 16 explores "The Call of the King," an exercise in the *Spiritual Exercises* of St. Ignatius, and how the call to transform the "kingdom" of today's society looks in the twenty-first century. The next chapter explores the ideas of compassion, both in Scripture and in the etymology of the word itself. The final chapter explores the application of outcomes language to immersive service. In other words, can we discuss some of the results of these experiences in a measurable way? For this exploration, the chapter draws upon Pedro Arrupe's iconic 1973 address, "Men and Women for Others."

Chapter 16

The Call of the King

Immersive service experiences can be very different based on the length of time, the location, and group dynamics. But although it is impossible to speak universally about every service experience, there are some outcomes that are likely across the board. One of the most substantial outcomes of being involved in a service experience could be the new, or renewed, awareness of injustice and oppression in the world. Perhaps you now have a new boy-with-bread moment, a time when you discovered that the reality of life for another person is not what you expected. These awakenings where you can say, "And now I see," could have been central or supplemental to the experience. For example, traveling to Immokalee taught me about the injustice of the immigration system and opened my eyes to the way of life for undocumented persons. It was a central component to the experience, and I had expected to learn about that topic on the trip. There were other things that I learned which I didn't anticipate. I grew in my understanding of the challenges of the education system, the process of manufacturing fruits and vegetables, and the plight of those living on the streets in Immokalee. Immersion and service work usually teach participants far more than they expected to learn.

For Christians, working for justice is hopefully intimately tied to one's prayer life and desire to follow Christ. One of the fruits of the previously mentioned *Spiritual Exercises* is to allow the internal revelations about God and oneself to transform one's behavior following the retreat. While there is extensive literature about living out the insights of the *Spiritual Exercises*, I want to focus on one example. Theologian Monika Hellwig, in her essay "The Call of the King and Justice," explores the application of the Kingdom exercise, which is found at the start of the second week of the Exercises. Although there are many meditations that could hit upon the theme of justice, exploration of the Kingdom (also known as the Call of the King) builds upon the discussion in part one of the Principle and Foundation. As Michael Ivens, SJ, a scholar of the *Spiritual Exercises*, points out, "[The Kingdom] can be described as a second Principle and Foundation."[78] So, as we explore this passage and Hellwig's insights, I hope you will keep in mind the formation of your own principle and foundation when you began this book and how those ideas may have been transformed by your participation in an immersive service experience.

The second week of the *Spiritual Exercises* invites retreatants to come to know Jesus by meditating on his life from infancy to the Passion. In his introductory anno-

---

78. Michael Ivens, S.J., *Understanding the Spiritual Exercises* (Trowbridge: Cromwell Press, 1998), 77.

tations describing the dual processes of week two, Ivens explains, "First, ongoing growth into the true life taught by Christ; second, the process of seeking and finding and responding to God's here-and-now word, i.e. election."[79] In other words, you come to know Christ so you can choose to follow Christ. The meditations begin, however, not with the birth of Jesus, but with a reflection on an imagined temporal king who is "chosen by God our Lord himself, whom all Christian princes and all Christian persons reverence and obey."[80] Ignatius then instructs that, in our imagination, we should observe this king and how he speaks, ultimately leading us to labor with the king toward his goals. This results in the formation of good subjects who have answered the call of the king chosen by God.

Hellwig explains the importance of the kingdom in the retreat and how it connects to discerning a call for social justice work. Regarding the meditation, she writes, "Ignatius takes no chance that the retreatant might miss the immediacy of the Gospel call for personal involvement. . . . By proposing the Kingdom meditation at the beginning, Ignatius places the entire week within a frame of reference of the worldwide crisis."[81] We are called to action by the cause of justice, represented by the king who calls us to

---

79. Ivens, *Understanding the Exercises*, 74.
80. Ignatius, "Spiritual Exercises," [92].
81. Monika Hellwig, "The Call of the King and Justice" in *The Way of Ignatius Loyola: Contemporary Approaches to the Spiritual Exercises* (Great Britain: SPCK, 1991), 81.

stand with him. In the call to fight against the injustices in the world we cannot wait.

Hellwig believes this exercise is also meant to challenge retreatants to look inward. She explains, "In terms of the issues named in the Second Week of the *Spiritual Exercises*, the underlying problem . . . is the inordinate human hunger for wealth, honour and power (pride)."[82] Combating these tendencies can be difficult, because the desires to be known, to be admired, and to have control over one's destiny are powerful lures. However, the call of Christ is toward poverty, being thought of with contempt, and powerlessness.[83] This does not mean one should simply cast aside all financial privileges or donate one's life savings. Nor does it mean not trying to achieve a degree in school that enables one to earn a comfortable living. Rather, it speaks to a reliance, putting God first, which will lead us to create a better world for others through justly using our privilege and resources. Jesus' example points the way for us to respond to the potential inordinate attachments of our interior life by outwardly living in a new way. This way seeks to create a more just and sustainable world for all of God's people.

The *Spiritual Exercises* is a formative experience. One of the key moments of the retreat is an encounter with Christ where we listen to what Christ reveals to us. The Kingdom meditation begins this process with the dichotomy between the king who follows Christ and the alternative—to live in the world ignoring Christ's call. As

---

82. Hellwig, "Call of the King," 77.
83. Hellwig, "Call of the King," 78.

Hellwig concludes, "These guidelines for making choices are applicable not only to individuals in decisions affecting their personal lives, but to communal action for social justice and the alleviation of mass suffering."[84] The choices you are making should not be seen only as spiritual reflections, but as having implications in the wider world.

In light of Hellwig's perspective of transformation toward working for justice, the rest of this chapter will offer specific examples of some of the most pressing issues in our country and our world. One of the ways to answer the question of how one should act following an intensive immersive experience is to allow it to bear fruit. A week in Immokalee or a year in Micronesia is not something that stays in that location. It is actually the opposite of the popular phrase, "What happens in Vegas, stays in Vegas." An immersion has the power to influence the decisions you make every day. You have been called by the King to change the Kingdom by the way you live.

Living in the Kingdom

In part five I offered the asymptote as an image for comprehending what it means to grow toward solidarity with another. I believe that direct immersion and postgraduate volunteer experiences are often the best way to grow closer

---

84. Hellwig, "Call of the King," 84.

to the asymptote, or, in other words, to become closer to another person. That growth should lead to action. In the next chapter we will explore the meaning of *compassion*, but before that, I want to offer a look at some of the issues affecting the world now and reflect on how immersion experiences can invite us to work toward solutions to these problems. If this is not the result of immersive service work, it is hard to argue against the perspective of Ivan Illich in part three, who chided immersion participants for being self-centered, opportunistic, or simply ignorant. Lessons from immersions must grow forth or the tree of justice could atrophy and your experiences be relegated to the pages of a scrapbook.

One of my current research projects is interviewing faculty and staff at John Carroll University about their experiences in immersion programs.[85] Although immersion programs are not geared toward these adult non-student participants, our initial studies indicate that chaperones, especially those who did not undergo an immersion as an undergraduate, are affected just as much as the students. Conducting these interviews in the spring and summer of 2020 meant that a number of respondents referred to what was going on in the country and in the world in their responses. Several important causes currently need attention in the United States and could be connected to immersion experiences, such as climate change, equal

---

85. The project includes Dr. Rich Clark and Dr. Anne McGinness from John Carroll University and will soon be expanded to include Vanessa Rotondo at Fordham University as well as contacts at other Jesuit universities.

treatment of and opportunities for women, respect for LGBTQIA individuals, reform of the immigration system, gun violence, respectful treatment of Native Americans, religious tolerance, abortion, and the death penalty, to name just a few. I want to focus on racism and COVID-19 as examples of the "twin pandemic" that faces the United States in the early 2020s. We are called to respond to the challenge presented in the Kingdom exercise. I hope to use the insights of the John Carroll chaperones as a springboard to reflect on how immersions can be a vehicle for change in this country.

In one interview, an adult who traveled with students on an immersion based on exploring the dynamics of racial justice stated, "I learned so much in terms of the treatment of formerly enslaved individuals. I learned so much about these atrocities . . . that opened my eyes to dynamics around power that I had not thought about. Things very relevant now in our public sphere. The realization that I thought I was educated and there was still so much I did not know." Also reflecting on racial power dynamics, another interviewee reflected, "Systems are real. Not just someone who had a bad roll of the dice. They might say they did, but these things are not accidental . . . so we are talking about racism. The concept of how justice plays out on a big scale."

In both cases, the participants drew upon their experiences in immersions and applied them to their growing awareness of racial inequality. The second respondent described how a student of color had participated in an immersion and used social media to encourage her group to join Black Lives Matter protests after the murder of George Floyd. To the chaperone's chagrin, there were few students who saw the connection between their immersion and this student's call for support. In his interview he lamented that immersions need to focus on sustaining the call for justice that is introduced during the immersive experience. It should be impossible to spend a week learning about unjust racial power dynamics and not see how these dynamics are connected to the deaths of Michael Brown, Tamir Rice, Freddie Gray, Eric Garner, and so many others who died before George Floyd. Making these connections does not mean all police officers or all white people want to harm Black people. It *does* mean that we are called to be agents of change, to work to prevent racist actions and undo racist systems. The weakest aspect of immersions, according to the over one hundred faculty and staff members we interviewed, revolved around the application of the experience upon the return. Allowing the experience to change you is the first and most basic way to honor the immersive service. At this point in the history of our country, racial injustices demand action.

The COVID pandemic of 2020 is another issue requiring an urgent response. The virus has affected the life of every woman, man, and child in the world in some way. It has also led to violence toward Asians, whom some erroneously hold responsible. These attacks have no basis in fact and continue to perpetuate the marginalization of Asian Americans in the United States. To this point, there has not been enough time to establish a structured immersion to explore the devastation caused by the pandemic. When the pandemic subsides, immersion programs should incorporate reflection on how different populations, in the United States and abroad, have been affected: for example, looking at the disparity of treatment and the rate of vaccination for communities of color, or the socioeconomic impacts of wealthier countries receiving more and/or quicker access to the vaccines. These are the types of realities that should be questioned as immersions begin anew. The COVID pandemic offers humanity a unique opportunity to see the ways that all people in the world are connected. How we act on that information will reveal much about the soul of humanity.

When Hellwig wrote her essay in the 1990s she named "world hunger, armaments race, nuclear threat, and racial violence" as issues facing the world. While these are still issues, the world has changed since her essay and will continue to change in the twenty-first century. Working for the Kingdom of God, answering the call for justice, is an ongoing and transforming endeavor. Immersive service work should not only teach us how to respond to an injustice in the moment, but should also give us the tools to look ahead and anticipate when someone will be in need. Going on an immersion or doing postgraduate volunteer service does not mean you are perfect in your understanding of social justice. We should always continue to learn, explore, and humbly enter into conversations about realities that are not our own. However, these experiences should at least make you more attuned to what is happening in the world. Now that we have discussed ways to honor your experience through action, we will turn in the next chapter to exploring ways to describe the encounter with others.

Reflection Questions

1. Pick one or two issues that are most prominent from your service experience. How do you think knowledge of these issues or a relationship with those who have suffered marginalization in these ways will help you to be more active in this area following your immersion? Create a concrete plan for how you can make a sustained commitment toward action.

2. What do you think are the three most important issues of justice today? Do you think that other members of your immersion or service community would agree with your list? How might your personal narrative (or theirs) impact the formation of this list?

Chapter 17

Filled with Compassion at the Sight

A few years ago my friend Nicole called me at 3:00 a.m. I usually have my phone on silent, but this particular night the ringer had been on high when I fell asleep. I awoke disoriented as she told me she was driving to the emergency veterinarian. Her kitten, Noah, was unable to breath and was choking. I knew how much she loved Noah. The panic in her voice was evident as I tried to keep her calm enough to drive safely. When she arrived at the vet she told me she would call me as soon as she could and hung up. Time passed slowly as I lay in bed awaiting news. The next time we spoke she said Noah had a heart condition and that the doctor recommended putting him to sleep because he was suffering and there was nothing they could do. I tried to be a suffering presence to her, despite the fact that we were hundreds of miles apart. She hung up so she could be with her kitten in his final moments.

I didn't have a pet growing up. I interacted with Noah two or three times and while he was a cute and playful kitten, I did not form a strong connection to him. I was surprised, therefore, at how painful the next few days were for me. In a way, I was not suffering because Noah had been put to sleep. I was suffering because someone I cared about was suffering. While there are other examples I could use that involved the death of a human being, I chose to use the story of Nicole's cat because I did not have an inclination toward her pet. When Lisa died of cancer, I suffered with her family. When Mac died by suicide, I suffered with his family. In both cases, I also grieved the loss of the person who had died and what the person meant to *my* life. The loss of Noah did not impact my life directly, yet I suffered. I want to be clear: I am not saying the death of a human being is the same as the death of a cat. At the same time, all life is sacred. Loss of life in any form may set us on a path of grief and suffering. I am simply highlighting the third-party experience of suffering because another person is suffering.

The process I just described is the meaning of the word *compassion*. Derived from the Latin word *compassio*, compassion literally means "to suffer with." In Luke 15, the father of the prodigal son was moved with compassion. The father suffered when he saw the condition of the wayward youth. Pope Francis, in his homily at Lampedusa, says society has forgotten the meaning of compassion—we do not suffer with those dying on the boats. Their deaths do not move us in any way. Father Boyle, likewise, challenges us to invite people into the circle of compassion, into the place within the circle where all are connected. When one part of the circle suffers, all suffer. Cultivating the skills of compassion is another way to honor the experience of your immersion. That is the power of boundless compassion: the circle united around all people.

Go and Do Likewise

Another example of a Scripture parable that offers insight into compassion is the parable of the Good Samaritan in Luke 10:29–37. When Jesus is asked, "Who is my neighbor?" he replies with the now-famous tale of a man who is beaten and left on the side of the road. After a priest and a Levite pass by on the opposite side of the road, a Samaritan traveler is "moved with compassion at the sight" (NABRE). Once again, insight into Jesus' audience helps us understand the radical nature of this moment. They would have expected religious leaders to stop. A Samaritan, however, was the enemy to Jesus' audience. The Samaritan not only stops, but also "suffers with" the wounded traveler. Jesus has turned the narrative on its head and delivered an unexpected turn. But the man is not only moved with compassion emotionally. He takes care of the wounded man, sacrificing money and time to make sure he is okay. As the Samaritan takes his patient to an inn, he informs the innkeeper that he will return and offer more money if needed to make sure the man fully recovers. The Samaritan goes above and beyond what many would say is his obligation. The parable concludes with Jesus telling his listeners, "Go and do likewise."

Theologian William Spohn uses this statement as the central idea in his book *Go and Do Likewise: Jesus and Ethics*.

He writes, "'Pity' is a pallid translation of *esplangchnisthe*, which means being shaken in the depths of the womb or bowels, a wrenching gut reaction. The Samaritan has a visceral compassion for the man that goes beyond pity."[86] Spohn explains that compassion bridges the gap between what we see and the actions we take. It motivates us to move from awareness toward aid. Thus, when Jesus is answering the question concerning who is the man's neighbor, his response is to offer a parable where the Samaritan does not stop to think about who is his neighbor, but simply lets his heart be moved by the sight of suffering. Father Boyle's circle of compassion, for the Samaritan, is not bounded by tribal dispute. The circle knows only the suffering of a fellow human being.

Spohn's book can be categorized as a study in virtue ethics, which emphasizes the way Scripture can help in the formation of virtue. This perspective mirrors the comments of Hauerwas regarding the church and being a suffering presence from part four. Hauerwas claims that the Gospel teaches one how to be present to the dying. This is a form of virtue acquisition: learning presence in the way Jesus taught. Spohn explains, "An ethics of character and virtue offers the most adequate approach to the *story of scripture* because that story aims to transform not only our individual actions, but our 'hearts,' that is, the whole embodied person as related to others."[87] Studying

---

86. William C. Spohn, *Go and Do Likewise: Jesus and Ethics*, (New York: Continuum, 2003), 89.
87. Spohn, *Do Likewise* 12.

Scripture and entering into immersive service is not only an intellectual exercise, but an exercise of the heart that is transformative in nature.

"Go and do likewise" is perhaps a catchphrase for this part of the book. How should you honor your immersion experience? By allowing yourself to be moved with compassion at the sight, and then going and doing *as* the Samaritan traveler did. Act upon the stirrings of your heart, going above and beyond what is expected as you stand for justice and against those who would hurt innocent people. It is not enough to feel pity. When Asian Americans are attacked, when Black people are denied due process under the law, when LGBTQIA people are denied equality, when women are assaulted, when anyone is treated as disposable, Christians are called to go and do as the Samaritan did. Allow compassion to move you to action to protect the vulnerable. Hopefully, when you return from an immersion, you have had your heart formed as the Samaritan did. At the very least, it is hoped that you will not act as the priest and the Levite did, walking on the other side of the road and refusing to truly see the plight of others. When your heart is open you may find yourself suffering with the other, filled with compassion at the sight.

Reflection Questions

1. Have you ever had an experience where you were "moved with compassion" as I was for Nicole's suffering? Describe the situation and then spend time reflecting on the way you felt. How is "suffering with" different from pity or sadness?

2. What values or virtues have you formed during your immersive service experience? Are these now part of your non-negotiables? In other words, part of the fabric of who you are at your core? If so, what concrete actions might you now take in your life because of these new perspectives?

Chapter 18

Life-Changing Experiences

When my friend Molly returned to the United States from Ecuador she struggled to find her place. While serving for one year with *Rostro de Cristo* she could easily point to a purpose in each day. Working with children, being present to the neighbors, and living a life of intentionality were central to her experience abroad. Things became much more difficult when she returned to the United States. Ultimately, she decided to return to Ecuador to be a teacher for a few years. One might say she still had more to give to and more to learn from the people she left behind. Although rare, Molly's story is another example to counter the perspective of Illich. Illich believed those who serve in immersion experiences return to their home country without having fully immersed in the country they left behind. But for Molly, Ecuador had become a new home.

Earlier in part six I mentioned a research group that was interviewing faculty and staff who had participated in immersion programs. This project grew out of a previous one that surveyed nearly 450 John Carroll alumni who had participated in an immersion program five to fifteen years prior. Our research sought to explore if immersions were truly "life-changing," as students often report immediately following a short-term immersion. We felt that if former students reported "positive change" in a variety of categories, it would indicate the changes they experienced had a long-term effect on their lives. In short, we found that an overwhelming number of students reported that participation in immersions affected their actions or choices; their cognitive, emotional, and moral growth; their understanding of social responsibility; and their spiritual growth.[88]

As a faculty member who has accompanied students on service experiences, I was not surprised by some of the results, but I was impressed by the longitudinal aspect of these changes. Some people who had completed immersions ten to fifteen years prior still reported that those experiences played a role in where they shopped, how they viewed access to water, and how they understood information they read about or heard on the news. While these results alone do not offer evidence for the importance of continuing immersion programs or for engaging in postgraduate volunteer work, they do demonstrate that such changes are more than passing fancies that dissipate a few weeks after the experience.

One example from my time in Immokalee is the recognition of people as equal human beings, regardless of their

---

88. Richard Clark, Anne McGinness, James Menkhaus, and Andy Costigan, "Looking Five Years Post-Immersion: The Long-Term effects of Undergraduate Immersions," *Journal of Catholic Higher Education*, (38:1: 2019), 55–79.

documentation status. On my second trip to Immokalee I was walking along the street with a student named John. Some children were playing with a soccer ball on the other side of a fence when suddenly the ball landed at our feet. We smiled and waved to the kids as John reached down, picked up the ball, and tossed it over the fence to them. In that moment, John smiled, looked at me, and said, "These are people too." John's insight has always stayed with me because it was such a beautiful moment of metanoia. It is not that John would have said the children were not people prior to the ball sailing over the fence. John is a caring person who believed all people had human dignity before he spoke these words. It is the innocence of the reaction. In that moment his heart was touched; the curve inched closer to the asymptote of solidarity in a new way. It was a moment of graced solidarity. It has been nearly ten years since that immersion trip, but John and I both remember it clearly and as a moment of special insight.

Immokalee has also been a place where many of my students have come to understand that being undocumented does not make a person illegal. The use of the term "illegals" by the news or by people in conversation devalues the personhood of those individuals. A person can do an illegal action, like border crossing, speeding, or underage drinking. However, when someone is pulled over for going fifteen miles per hour over the speed limit, or college students are in the news for hazing another student with alcohol and causing their death, they are not referred to as illegals. They are people who speed, or people who have made bad choices with alcohol. But when people choose to cross the border without documentation, apparently some in the news media think they lose their humanity. They are now illegal humans. This is one of the first lessons students who travel to Immokalee learn. When they hear their friends or family refer to people as "illegals" they can do their best to educate others about the difference between an illegal action and the person who takes it. They honor the experience in Immokalee by speaking the truth about the marginalized and they affirm that "these are people too."

In addition to my own memories that I have recalled in the book so far, I wish to offer one more example that has stayed with me. While in Honduras we visited a boy suffering from a variety of medical conditions. People would visit with him and hold his hand or sit by his bedside, but we were told that he did not have long to live and that the possibilities for medical care were so diminished in his village there was nothing they could do to help him, except make him feel more comfortable. As I sat near him, I thought of my own health. As a cystic fibrosis patient, I would have died if I were born in many other countries at that time. In the first three months of my life doctors tried numerous operations and new procedures to keep me alive. The life expectancy for a CF patient when I was born was less than five years. Medical advancements today have pushed the life expectancy over forty for those with CF living in the United States. Sitting with this child reminded me of my own privilege and opportunities for life that I have been given. These insights are personal but are also powerful and life changing.

Education for Others

In each part of this book you have read a short story or insight from Pedro Arrupe. Arrupe was responsible for employing the vision of the Second Vatican Council in the way he governed the Jesuits. From his experiences as a medical student encountering a young boy to his time as a missionary convicted of espionage and ministering to the victims of the atomic bomb, Arrupe's spirit was formed through encounters with others and in the depth of his prayer. To conclude the final part of this book, which is dedicated to honoring your immersive service experiences, I think it is appropriate to briefly explore some of the themes from his most famous speech as superior general of the Society of Jesus.

Arrupe delivered the speech on the Feast of St. Ignatius, July 31, 1973, in Valencia, Spain. Those gathered were Jesuit-educated alumni from around Europe, many from affluent backgrounds. Drawing upon the 1971 synod of bishops and their document "Justice in the World," Arrupe delivered a speech that both challenged and angered many in the audience. Perhaps his best-known speech, "Men and Women for Others" has since become a motto for Jesuit high schools and colleges around the world.

Early in the speech, Arrupe delivers the lines that have become catchphrases in Jesuit circles. He proclaims:

> "Today our prime educational objective must
> be to form men-and-women-for-others; men
> and women who will live not for themselves

but for God and his Christ—for the God-human who lived and died for all the world; men and women who cannot even conceive of love of God which does not include love for the least of their neighbors; men and women completely convinced that love of God which does not issue in justice for others is a farce."[89]

By challenging any notion that the faith does not call one to action, Arrupe establishes the mission of Jesuit education as forming people who will live for others. Life for others includes a life dedicated to Christ and to God, not to self-gain and personal achievement. Just as Christ sacrificed himself in love, this same love should be taught at Jesuit schools so alumni can become willing to give of themselves as Christ did. Particularly in need of this love are the poor and vulnerable in society. For one to say he or she loves God, but not to enact this love in the world, goes against Jesus' words in the Gospel and the love he showed to those he encountered. Arrupe's challenge to those who say they love God but do not love their neighbor remains central to Jesuit education today.

Arrupe then reflects on whether his audience, who had been educated in Jesuit schools, had been educated for justice. He responds to his own question: no, they have not. He states, "If the terms 'justice' and 'education for

---

89. Pedro Arrupe, S.J., "Men and Women For Others," in *Pedro Arrupe: Essential Writings*, introduction by Kevin Burke, S.J. and foreword Peter-Hans Kolvenbach, S.J. (Maryknoll, New York: Orbis Books, 2004), 173.

justice' carry all the depth and meaning which the church gives them today, we have not educated you for justice."[90] However, Arrupe believes that despite the work ahead to correct this problem, it can be accomplished. If Jesuit education teaches its graduates to be open to the signs of the times and to listen to the call of the Gospel, then the alumni will understand the importance the church places on education for justice.

The desire to educate for justice is not merely a Jesuit initiative, nor was Arrupe attempting to put forth his own agenda. He clearly traces his position back to the bishops' document "Justice in the World," which developed from the vision of Vatican II. These ideas come from Pope Paul VI's 1967 encyclical *Populorum progressio*; the 1968 meeting of Latin American bishops at Medellín, Colombia; the 1969 meeting of African bishops at Kampala, Uganda; the 1970 meeting of Asian bishops at Manila in the Philippines; and Paul VI's *Octogesima adveniens* in 1971.[91] The 1971 bishops' synod, however, took these positions even further. For these bishops, working on behalf of justice is a constitutive dimension of preaching the Gospel. Arrupe reflects, "We cannot, then, separate action for justice and liberation from oppression from the proclamation of the Word of God."[92]

This love for others demonstrated through action for justice is connected with the love of God as well. Given Jesus' words in Matthew 25 that how one treats the least in

---

90. Arrupe, "Men and Women," 173.
91. Arrupe, "Men and Women," 176.
92. Arrupe, "Men and Women," 177.

society is how one treats Christ, and given who Jesus spent his time with—the poor, oppressed, and outcast—it is clear that one's love of God is connected to one's love of others. If Christians are called to love all people, as Christ commanded them, then this love must be connected to justice. Arrupe states, "Take justice away from love and you destroy love. You do not have love if the beloved is not seen as a person whose dignity must be respected, with all that that implies."[93] Protecting human dignity is strongly connected to loving the other person. One cannot be said to love the other person if one ignores how their human dignity is violated or how justice is denied them. And if one does not love the other, and does not work for the dignity of others, one cannot be sure one's love of God is authentic.

Arrupe continues by explaining what he means by works of justice, which should go beyond an individual's actions. First, he means an attitude of respect toward people, where persons are not treated as a means to profit. Second, people should never be oppressed by positions of power derived from privilege, because to do so "even passively, is equivalent to active oppression." Arrupe strongly contends, "To be drugged by the comforts of privilege is to become contributors to injustice as silent beneficiaries of the fruits of injustice." And third, Arrupe advocates an attitude that not only refuses injustice, but also counterattacks it. This position should involve "a decision to work with others toward the dismantling of unjust social structures

---

93. Arrupe, "Men and Women," 178.

so that the weak, the oppressed, the marginalized of this world may be set free."[94] Ignoring injustice or allowing it to happen contributes to it by not standing against it.

Although some may contend that Christianity is about individual freedom from sin and not social sin, Arrupe sees these as connected. Purification from one's inner sins is not separated from the social sin that exists rampantly today. Purification of the world is also the call of Christ. Arrupe explains, "God's grace calls us not only to win back our whole selves for God, but to win back our whole world for God. We cannot separate personal conversion from structural social reform."[95] Just because the efforts of those working for justice will never be fully accomplished in this world does not mean that the fight should not be fought.

Arrupe ends his speech by describing how the church needs women and men for others, people who hear the call to go outside themselves and to give themselves in love. Arrupe states, "Only those who love fully realize themselves as persons."[96] He contrasts this with egoism, those who dehumanize themselves through reckless ambition, competition, and self-destruction. Dehumanization of oneself leads to the dehumanization of others as people exploit others for their own gain and power. Egoism has its roots in a denial of love, which is the very core of the Christian

94. Arrupe, "Men and Women," 179.
95. Arrupe, "Men and Women," 181.
96. Arrupe, "Men and Women," 183.

message.[97] In order to fight this egoism, people should not fight evil with evil, but with good instead.

While this will be difficult, Arrupe offers three attitudes to cultivate in a person's life to overcome egoism. First, he says to live more simply. This will slow down the trending tide of consumerism and luxurious living spurred through social competition. To this point, he says, "Men and women who, instead of feeling compelled to acquire everything that their friends have will do away with many of the luxuries which in their social set have become necessities, but which the majority of humankind must do without."[98] Second, people should not draw profit from an unjust source. Instead, they should work to reduce privilege in favor of the underprivileged. And third, they should commit themselves to be agents of change in society. This does not mean simply "resisting unjust structures and arrangements, but actively undertaking to reform them."[99] Again, ignoring an injustice makes one a party to it, which devalues human dignity and Christian love. Arrupe calls his audience to be men and women for others, in order to become fully human themselves, because it is only in loving others, as Christ commanded, that one becomes a full person.

Arrupe's description of the outcomes of a true Jesuit education can be adapted to the outcomes of a postgraduate volunteer or immersion experience. How have you changed in your desire for self-gain or influence? How have

97. Arrupe, "Men and Women," 184.
98. Arrupe, "Men and Women," 185.
99. Arrupe, "Men and Women," 186.

you changed in the way you see others and unjust social structures that keep people from being able to live a life of equality? Can you now say, in a new way, "These are people too," and affirm that all people have human dignity? Have you changed in the way you judge others, acknowledging that it is not only circumstances that cause people to be in a difficult situation, but also systems of power and privilege that actively seek to deny the equality of all people? Wrestling with these questions is how you honor your experience. Let your heart be moved with compassion and let your education about the world lead you to make this world a better place.

Reflection Questions

1. What outcomes can you concretely describe following your experience? If you had to defend your program to a donor who wishes to see "evidence" of growth in you and your group, what can you offer as proof of transformation?

2. Arrupe's "Men and Women for Others" speech connects internal transformation with a desire for justice. Do you agree with him that these ideas work hand in hand? If so, give examples for yourself from your own service journey.

Conclusion

The Rest Is Still Unwritten

When I was in middle school I remember sitting in an assembly. We had a speaker who was trying to inspire us to be "better citizens" or something along those lines. I only remember one thing about that talk, but it is a piece of advice that has stayed with me many years later. The presenter told us, "I am not everyone, so I can't do everything. But I am someone, so I can do something." I remember this advice when I become overburdened by the injustices I witness on the news or the pain I see in people I care about. I think about this when I return from an immersion program with a new fire to make a difference, only to find that a short time later I am busy with the daily routines of life and become disenchanted with myself for not doing more. I try to remember this when I want to change the world and find that I cannot even change those around me. I am not everyone, so I can't do everything. But I am someone, so I can do something.

As this book concludes, I feel it is important to offer a few concrete ways to honor the experience that you have had. First, let the experience change you in some way. Pick something about your service that you want to integrate into the non-negotiable values of who you are. Perhaps it's the formation of a new principle and foundation for your ethical compass. Hopefully you are not entirely the same as you were prior to the experience. Second, continue to learn about what you have witnessed. Do research, continue the conversation, seek out other opportunities to grow and learn. The experience should be the beginning of a new chapter, not the conclusion. Third, for those who have completed a short-term immersion, consider postgraduate volunteer service. This may not be the best path for everyone. Pray about it. Be open to it. Many volunteers I have worked with have told me the possibility of doing such a program developed over time and was not something they anticipated at the start of their collegiate career. Fourth, identify concrete ways to act. Increasing community service of some sort, even if it is not directly related to the population or cause you worked with during your immersive experience, will continue to keep the spark of service alive in your heart. Fifth, continue to pray about how the Holy Spirit may call you in the future. Whether you had an amazing experience or really struggled, remain open. Praying the Examen after you return from your experience will help you be aware of small and large ways to continue to honor the experience by being in tune with the movements of the Spirit in your life.

If you return from an immersive service experience and nothing changes, it is possible that Ivan Illich is correct. The experience did not have a lasting impact and the money may have been better spent directly helping others. It is rare that I have seen someone return from an immersion and not make short-term changes in their life. The difficulty is keeping those changes for the long term, making them part of who you are at your core. Letting your heart be moved with compassion at the sight. But that is up to you.

The rest is still unwritten because that is *your* story. If you were to write this book, what conversations would you include? What concepts do you think are important in immersion work to help you truly respect the people you might encounter? You have been given a great privilege to walk with and encounter people who have been marginalized in some way by society. You have been given a great gift. Therefore, you have the responsibility to embody that gift and to cherish it. I am forever grateful to Moncho, the most selfless *profesor* I have ever met, for teaching me this lesson.

Your Heart Has Been Formed

The introduction to this book began by recalling a homily by Father Gray in which he shared about the elderly nun who inspired him to give his heart to God every day of his life. She reflected that it can appear easy to give your hands to God through service or your mind to God in teaching and learning. But she challenged Father Gray to not get caught up in "doing" things for the Kingdom of God to such an extent that "being" with God is sacrificed. While this book focused a lot on the "promotion of justice," I hope it did not neglect the "service of faith." These two concepts are intertwined in Ignatian spirituality and in the lived witness of Pedro Arrupe. It is my hope that after reading this text and reflecting on its material that your life can, in your own way, embody this balance as well.

I would like to offer another homily by Father Gray as a bookend. In May 2007 he delivered a baccalaureate homily at John Carroll. His homily reflects on the formation provided by a Jesuit education and is equally applicable to a woman or man who is returning from an intensive immersion experience or postgraduate volunteer program.

His words embody much of what I hope this book has achieved, so I will include a lengthy excerpt. As you read it, I invite you to imagine that the audience is not a graduating class who will soon receive a diploma, but instead you, returning from a transformative and potentially life-changing immersive experience.

> When Christ Jesus ascends to the Father he brings a love that has no ending, for people where they are, as they are . . . so that the whole texture of the human family has been blessed and brought before the Father because every part of everyone he met became part of him. . . . And if we asked him, Jesus what do you leave this world? Where is your library? Where is your lab? Where is your corporation? Where is your entourage, or, at least where is your plan? He comes empty handed. 'I have nothing, except those who followed me.' Therefore, he will continue to be who he is through who they are. Now they must go forth and they must witness to all that he was and taught. . . . Given that reality, through the window of Christ, what if we peer in the other side and I say, what is the window of reality into a graduate of John Carroll? The reality is, the greatest gift you can give to God is yourself, who you are. Your mind has been honed, trained, . . . your hands have been given skills, . . . but far more important is what has happened to your

heart. How has that been touched? We like to feel that it has been touched so that when you leave this school your heart will ache every time you see some kid going to bed at night hungry and you will be outraged when you see anyone in this society ostracized and marginalized because of their race, their color, or their gender preference. *That is not the way of Christ.* You have been told and you have been entrusted to bear that witness of Christ that in the Kingdom of God there are no outcasts. The net is wide and strong and it will gather together many and I want to be one of the workers that pull it to shore.[100]

How has your heart been formed by your experience? How will you move forward in your life in light of these realizations? This is the work of the Kingdom of God. Hopefully your service experience has touched your heart and honed you to be attentive to the suffering of others, especially those living on the margins of society. You are the one to continue to bear witness to the Gospel. You are the one entrusted to pull the nets ashore with the bounty of equality and acceptance. In the wake of the lessons learned during 2020 from the COVID-19 pandemic and the racial inequality that is endemic to our country, the need could scarcely be greater for leaders to step up

---

100. Howard Gray, S.J., Homily Delivered at John Carroll University, May 19, 2007.

and chart a new path forward. Our world needs those who refuse to patronize disadvantaged persons through photos, who have served as a suffering presence to those who have been discarded, and who have inched toward the asymptote of solidarity. You do not need to achieve perfection to tell the stories of what you have witnessed and to allow your heart to be transformed. You only need to strive to live authentically, rooted in Gospel love, and to honor what you have experienced in the way you live your life. On the pilgrimage of service, come as you are. In the end, give your heart to God, because the greatest gift you can give to God is yourself.

Bibliography

Arrupe, S.J., Pedro. *Justice with Faith Today.* Edited by Jerome Aixala S.J. St. Louis: The Institute of Jesuit Sources, 1980.

———— *One Jesuit's Spiritual Journey: Autobiographical Conversations with Claude Dietsch, S.J.* Translated by Ruth Bradley. St. Louis: The Institute of Jesuit Sources, 1986.

———— *Other Apostolates Today,* ed. Jerome Aixala, S.J. St. Louis: The Institute of Jesuit Sources, 1981.

———— *Pedro Arrupe: Essential Writings.* Edited by Kevin Burke. New York: Orbis Books, 2004.

———— *Recollections and Reflections of Pedro Arrupe, S.J.* Translated by Yolanda T. De Mola and with an introduction by Vincent O'Keefe. Wilingham, DE: Michael Glazier, 1986.

Barron, Robert. *And Now I See: A Theology of Transformation.* New York: Crossroad Publishing, 1998.

Bishop, George D. *Pedro Arrupe, S.J.: Twenty-Eighth General of the Society of Jesus.* Leominster: Gracewing, 2007. Anand, Gujarat, India: Gujarat Sahitya Prakash, 2000.

Boyle, S.J., Greg. *Tattoos on the Heart: The Power of Boundless Compassion.* New York: Free Press, 2010.

Clark, Richard, Anne McGinness, James Menkhaus, and Andy Costigan. "Looking Five Years Post-Immersion: The Long-Term Effects of Undergraduate Immersions." *Journal of Catholic Higher Education.* 38, no. 1 (2019).

Gallagher, Timothy. *The Examen Prayer: Ignatian Wisdom for Our Lives Today.* New York: Crossroad Publishing, 2006.

Gray, S.J., Howard. Baccalaureate Homily, John Carroll University, May 2007.

Hauerwas, Stanley. *Suffering Presence: Theological Reflections on Medicine, the Mentally Handicapped, and the Church.* Notre Dame, IN: University of Notre Dame Press, 1986

Hellwig, Monika. "The Call of the King and Justice." In *The Way of Ignatius Loyola: Contemporary Approaches to the Spiritual Exercises,* edited by Philip Sheldrake, 77-85. London: SPCK, 1991.

Ignatius. *Ignatius of Loyola: Spiritual Exercises and Selected Works.* Edited by George E. Gnass New York: Paulist Press, 1991.

Illich, Ivan. "To Hell with Good Intentions." Address to the Conference on InterAmerican Student Projects, Cuernavaca, Mexico, April 20, 1968. *www.uvm. edu/~jashman/CDAE195_ESCI375/To%20Hell%20 with%20Good%20Intentions.pdf.*

Ivens, Michael. *Understanding the Spiritual Exercises.* Trowbridge, Wiltshire: Cromwell Press, 1998.

Kolvenbach, Peter-Hans. "The Service of Faith and the Promotion of Justice in American Jesuit Higher Education." In *A Jesuit Education Reader,* edited by George W. Traub, 144-62. Chicago: Loyola Press, 2008.

Kurtz, Ernest, and Katherine Ketcham. *The Spirituality of Imperfection: Storytelling and the Search for Meaning.* New York: Bantam Books, 1993.

Kushner, Harold. *When Bad Things Happen to Good People.* New York: Shocken Books, 1989.

Lamet, Pedro Miguel. *Pedro Arrupe: Witness of the Twentieth Century, Prophet of the Twenty-First.* Boston College: Institute of Jesuit Sources, 2020.

Lewis, S.J., Hedwig. *Pedro Arrupe Treasury.* Gujarat, India: Gujarat Sahitya Prakash, 2007.

Martin, S.J., James. *Learning to Pray: A Guide for Everyone.* New York: Harper One, 2021.

Manney, Jim. *A Simple Life-Changing Prayer: Discovering the Power of St. Ignatius Loyola's Examen.* Chicago: Loyola Press, 2001.

Modras, Ronald. *Ignatian Humanism: A Dynamic Spirituality for the 21st Century.* Chicago: Loyola Press, 2004.

Francis. *Evangelii Gaudium: On the Proclamation of the Gospel in Today's World.* Vatican City: Libreria Editrice Vaticana, November 24, 2013.

———— "Homily of the Holy Father Francis." Homily given on his visit to Lampedusa, July 8, 2013. *www.vatican.va/content/francesco/en/homilies/2013/ documents/papa-francesco_20130708_omelia-lampedusa.html.*

Riley, O.P., Maria. "Feminist Analysis: A Missing Perspective." In *The Logic of Solidarity: Commentaries on Pope John Paul II's Encyclical 'On Social Concern.'* Edited by Gregory Baum and Robert Ellsberg. Maryknoll, New York: Orbis Books, 1989.

Spohn, William C. *Go and Do Likewise: Jesus and Ethics.* NY: Continuum, 2003.

Wallace, SJ, Frank. "Prayer as Encounter and Not Performance." In *Encounter Not Performance*, 3-8. Newton, Australia: E.J. Dwyer, 1991.

New City Press

New City Press is one of more than 20 publishing houses sponsored by the Focolare, a movement founded by Chiara Lubich to help bring about the realization of Jesus' prayer: "That all may be one" (John 17:21). In view of that goal, New City Press publishes books and resources that enrich the lives of people and help all to strive toward the unity of the entire human family. We are a member of the Association of Catholic Publishers.

www.newcitypress.com
202 Comforter Blvd.
Hyde Park, New York

Periodicals
Living City Magazine
www.livingcitymagazine.com

Scan to join our mailing list
for discounts and promotions
or go to www.newcitypress.com
and click on "join our email list."